KOKILA
An imprint of Penguin Random House LLC, New York

First published in the United States of America by Kokila,
an imprint of Penguin Random House LLC, 2023

Visit us online at penguinrandomhouse.com.

Library of Congress Cataloging-in-Publication Data

Names: Kendi, Ibram X., author. | Stone, Nic, author.
Title: How to be a (young) antiracist | by Dr. Ibram X. Kendi and Nic Stone.
Description: New York: Kokila, an imprint of Penguin Random House LLC, 2022.
Audience: Ages: 12–15 | Audience: Grades: 7–9 | Summary:
"The #1 New York Times bestseller that sparked international
dialogue is now a book for young adults! Based on the adult bestseller
by Ibram X. Kendi, and co-authored by bestselling author Nic Stone,
How to Be a (Young) Antiracist will serve as a guide for teens seeking a way forward in
acknowledging, identifying, and dismantling racism and injustice"— Provided by publisher.
Identifiers: LCCN 2022000891 | ISBN 9780593461600 (hardcover) |
ISBN 9780593461624 (ebook)
Subjects: LCSH: Anti-racism—United States—Juvenile literature. |
Youth—Political activity—United States—Juvenile literature. |
Racial justice—United States—Juvenile literature.
Classification: LCC E184.A1 .K343 2022 | DDC 305.800973—dc23/eng/20220615
LC record available at https://lccn.loc.gov/2022000891.

Manufactured in Canada

ISBN 9780593461600

1 3 5 7 9 10 8 6 4 2
FRI

ISBN 9780593529232 (INTERNATIONAL EDITION)
1 3 5 7 9 10 8 6 4 2

Design by Jasmin Rubero

Text set in Amasis MT Pro with Handelson Family

This is a work of nonfiction. Some names and identifying details have been changed.

For the foolishly optimistic.
We <u>will</u> win. Eventually.

—I. X. K. and N. S.

A Brief Word before We Begin . . .

As I'm sure you've deduced from that whole "Inspired by the #1 *New York Times* bestseller *How to Be an Antiracist*" statement on the cover, this book is . . . inspired by the #1 *New York Times* bestseller *How to Be an Antiracist*, the paradigm-shifting memoir written by Dr. Ibram X. Kendi.

And the *inspired by* is very important. Because *this* book is structured differently than its source of inspiration. Hence me, your beloved narrator, Nic Stone, including this *pre*-intro as a bit of a road map for the nonlinear journey you're about to take through Dr. Kendi's life.

Said journey is broken up into three parts (or *acts*, if we want to get all narratively fancy with it):

INSIDE: Facing Yourself

The concepts covered here—definitions, dueling consciousness, power, biology, behavior, Black, and White—are all about turning inward and are focused on examining the paradigms, aka foundational thoughts and ideas, that form our views of ourselves and other people.

OUTSIDE: Facing the World

Once we've done some self-examination and rejiggering, it'll be time to turn outward and take a microscopic-level look into the ways that racism permeates the world we live in and intersects with other forms of people being awful to each other. We're talking color, ethnicity, body, gender, orientation, class, culture, and space.

UPSIDE DOWN: Flipping the World Over

This is where we get about that action, boss. We're moving from failure to success and digging into what *I*—Nic—call the Four C's of Changemaking: cogency, compassion, creativity, and collaboration. We'll also make sure we have a solid grip on the power of pushing forward in spite of obstacles. And I know that a lot of you readers feel like you're ready to *get out there* and *tear down* the vile walls of racism, so, like, why not just jump to this section first, right?

Well, you *could*, obviously . . .

But in my humble opinion, it would behoove you to read the other two sections first.

Because as you, dear reader, will come to discover, being antiracist is more than a quick and easy decision you make. (And you don't have to make it right now, by the way. Do yourself—and the world—a favor by reading the book first.)

Being antiracist is . . . Well, I won't spoil it.

Just buckle up and get ready for the ride.

BEGINNING IN THE MIDDLE: YOUR (RACIST) INTRODUCTION

The year is 2000, and you, Ibram X. Kendi, are seventeen years old.

You hate wearing suits. And ties.

Hate it.

Today, though, you're in a suit *and* tie—black button-down, black slacks, golden-brown blazer, slick boots the color of the half-and-half you've seen adults pour into coffee, and the brightest, boldest tie you could find. You're also standing somewhere you never expected to be, about to do something you never expected to do.

It's your senior year of high school, and you're mere months from graduation. Getting *there* felt like a hard-fought battle with one arm tied behind your back. So being *here*? In this chapel with upward of three *thousand* people seated in rows that curve around the long, arched pulpit, all waiting to hear what YOU have to say? Flanked by two other Black high schoolers also dressed to the nines and waiting for their turns at the mic?

Yeah, this feels real good.

It's the perfect cap to a series of events that turned your world—both outer and inner, your sense of yourself and your capabilities—completely upside down. True, your competitors in the final round of the Prince William County Martin Luther King Jr. Oratorical Contest are a lot (book) smarter than you are. They certainly get better grades than the ones that make up your sub-3.0 GPA. And their SAT scores are hundreds of points higher than yours. You barely cracked 1000 . . .

But you are *here*, just like they are.

You won your high school oratorical competition, as you presume they did. You moved on to a countywide round, which they did as well. You were voted "best before the judge," which is how you wound up right here beside them on this makeshift stage.

And the best part: Just like them, you're headed to college.

Now, this might not *sound* like a huge deal—*obviously*, you're eventually going to college, right? Your parents both went, and from what you've heard, that's what all smart people do after graduating from high school. No-brainer.

The truth is, though, for a while you didn't feel very **smart**. You'd dropped out of your IB English class because you couldn't get your head around Shakespeare. *There's no way I'm smart enough for a university*, you thought.

But being on this stage isn't the first time you've been proven wrong about yourself. And as you'll soon come to discover, the fiery speech you're about to give is only the beginning.

The whole college thing had come as a huge surprise: A few weeks prior, you'd been minding your basketball business, running layup lines during a typical pre–home game warm-up session. Catch the pass, dribble forward, then gently leap and let the ball roll off your fingertips. Run to the opposite line and repeat.

But then the gym door opened, and in strode your dear ol' dad. Six-foot-three and two hundred pounds. Waltzed right onto the court, long arms waving to get your attention.

Your gut reaction: wide-eyed, breath-stopping embarrassment. As much as you love your pops, his blasé-blah attitude toward what you'll eventually come to call the "White judge"—a personified name for the overwhelming sense that power-bearing White people are evaluating your every move . . . something Dad couldn't care less about—really got under your skin back then. Prevent his true feelings from showing on his face? Nope. Keep his voice down? No way. Avoid making any sort of scene? Forget about it.

It scared you to have an African American father who lived by his own rules. It was the precise type of attitude that might've gotten him lynched in the past or shot down by a vigilante civilian or law enforcement official now.

But at any rate, there he was. So you jogged over to meet him.

He looked really geeked. Which was weird.

When you reached him, he handed you an envelope. Told you to open it. Like . . . right then and there at the half-court line before a game. With *everybody* watching. Including all the White people.

Of course, you complied.

It was an acceptance letter from Hampton University, one of the two colleges you'd applied to for the sole purpose of being able to say you'd tried.

That acceptance letter flipped your worldview on its head. Despite the test scores and report cards, you were smart enough to go to college after all. The other school you applied to, Florida A&M University, is the one you'll wind up attending, so you clearly got in there too (though you don't know that yet).

Standing on that court in front of your dad, a number of faulty ideas faded from your mind. So did your sense of what you would later come to know as the "White gaze." With that letter in your hand, the stuff you believed about "intelligence" being proven by grades and test scores? It lost a bit of its validity.

Granted, you've still got a lot of ideas to unlearn and replace. You're not yet a reader, but you will be soon. And eventually, you'll look back and see a number of things through a cleaner lens.

But this moment on the basketball court is one you won't forget. It's the moment you awaken to the idea of something . . . more.

Now back to the MLK oratorical contest. You're up first.

And before you begin, you should know: You'll come to recall the "speech" you're about to give with . . . the *opposite* of pride.

For now, though, you're fired up. Ready to roll. Primed and pumped to share what *you* think is an updated version of Dr. King's dream.

So you take your place, and you begin.

"What would be Dr. King's message for the millennium?

"Let's visualize an angry seventy-one-year-old Dr. King . . ."

[It was joyous, our emancipation from enslavement . . . But . . .]

"Now, one hundred thirty-five years later, the Negro is still not free . . .

"Our youth's minds are still in captivity!

"They* think it's okay to be those who are most feared in our society!

"They think it's okay not to think!

"They think it's okay to climb the high tree of pregnancy!

"They think it's okay to confine their dreams to sports and music!"

(Applause, applause, and more applause.)

"Their minds are being held captive, and our adults' minds are right there beside them.

"Because they somehow think that the cultural revolution that began on the day of my dream's birth is over.

"How can it be over when many times we are unsuccessful because we lack intestinal fortitude?"

*They as in Black youth.

(Everybody claps.)

"How can it be over when our kids leave their houses not knowing how to make themselves, only knowing how to not make themselves?"

(Everybody claps.)

"How can it be over if all of this is happening in our community?"

And then . . . with everyone at the edge of their seats, hanging on your every word, you drop your voice for the finale:

"So I say to you, my friends, that even though this cultural revolution may never be over,

"I still have a dream . . ."

And the crowd goes *wild*.

A crowd full of African American adults. (You're in a Black church, after all.)

Validation.

But the thing is . . . you're wrong. And everyone who agreed with you by way of applause is also wrong.

It'll take you some time to realize that your words aren't as virtuous as the resounding applause has made you believe they are. Eventually, you realize that it'll take more than a surprise pair of college admission letters and a spot in the finals of an oratorical contest to shift your sense of yourself and other Black people.

In this moment, though, with the approval of Black men, women, *and* children ringing in your ears, you don't realize it . . .

But everything you said is racist.

Later, you'll wonder: Was it your poor sense of yourself that generated your poor sense of your people? Or was it your poor sense of your people that fueled your poor sense of yourself?

Both were evident in that speech.

For instance . . .

You mentioned *our youth's minds* being "in captivity" . . . but what exactly are they in captivity to?

You mentioned Black youth's okay-ness with being feared . . . but is that their fault alone?

Your mentioned Black youth being cool with not thinking . . .

7

which is little more than a remix of the old adage that Black kids don't value education as much as their non-Black counterparts. But is that actually true?

Number three is particularly *insidious*—a word you'll come to use that basically means EVIL in a dastardly villain–type of way. Because it hasn't occurred to you that even *you* had fallen prey to the precise thing you were shouting down. Remember your shock at getting into not one, but *two* colleges? Said shock came from your belief that you were a lousy student. Thing is, that mess you spouted came from *mess*ages—from Black people, White people, and the media— that told you the lousiness was rooted in your race. That (naturally) put a damper on your motivation to put forth more effort, which then reinforced number three up there: Black people just aren't very studious.

On and on the cycle went because you'd bought that racist idea hook, line, and sinker. To the point where you were primed and ready to preach it—and the others—to a crowd full of Black people on MLK Day in the form of a revised "I Have a Dream" speech.

That's the thing about racist ideas: They make people of color think less of themselves . . . which makes them more vulnerable to racist ideas (these are **internalized racist ideas**, but we'll get to that later). And then on the flip side, the same racist ideas make White people think *more* of themselves, which further attracts them to racist ideas. And all of this tends to happen inside of people without anyone realizing it. Yourself included.

Because that's the goal of that dastardly villain, Racist Ideology: It manipulates us into thinking *people*—and therefore people *groups*— are the problem instead of the *policies* that perpetuate the racial inequities.

But we're getting ahead of ourselves.

What you need to know before we jump back in time to the *beginning* of your story:

- *Racism* is real and dastardly villainous, and denial is what keeps its ugly heart beating.
- *Racist* is more an adjective than a noun, and it's *not* an insult; anyone who *takes* it as an insult or tries to *use* it as one likely doesn't know what the word actually means.
- *Not racist* is not a thing in the fight for a more equitable world; there is *racist* and there is *antiracist*.
- *Color-blind* as applied to race is also not a thing; it, like *not racist*, is a part of the denial that keeps lifeblood pumping through that ugly and insidious heart of *racism*.

At this point in your life, you are racist most of the time. Yes, you read that right. You, IXK, a young *Black* man, currently subscribe to a *lot* of racist ideas.

But you won't forever. And that's what this book is about: the journey to being fully human and to seeing others as fully human.

And you will come to see the movement from *racist* to *antiracist* as always ongoing—requiring understanding and snubbing racism based on flawed ideas about biology, ethnicity, body, culture, behavior, color, space, and class—because antiracism also involves standing ready to fight at racism's intersections with other forms of prejudice and bigotry.

It's time to learn what it *truly* means to be **ANTIRACIST**.

Part One

INSIDE: FACING OURSELVES

I began to silence the war within me . . . and started
embracing the struggle toward a single
antiracist consciousness.

—Dr. Ibram X. Kendi, *How to Be an Antiracist*

DEFINITIONS: WHY THEY MATTER
(Just Like Black Lives Do)

In order to get you to that life-flipping speech, we gotta start *before* your beginning. Twelve years before. In 1970. It was then, at an InterVarsity Christian Fellowship conference called Urbana 70, that the woman and man who would become your mom and dad had *their* lives flipped.

For the first time ever, the second night of this Very Big Deal evangelical summit for college kids would be dedicated to Black theology.

What on earth is Black theology? you might be wondering.

Well, your parents, Carol and Larry, were wondering too. It's part of the reason they decided to even go—independent of each other— to Urbana 70. They'd heard that this really *groovy* band called Soul Liberation would be playing, and that the headlining preacher for Black theology night was this guy named Tom Skinner.

At that point, Skinner, a Harlem-born former gang member and the son of a Baptist preacher (which sounds like an oxymoron, I know) was growing in popularity as a champion of this thing called *Black liberation theology*. Your mom's introduction to Skinner's work was one of happenstance: She had a college classmate who happened to be Skinner's baby brother. And your dad stumbled into the guy's teachings after taking a college course that opened his eyes to a lot of stuff he hadn't noticed about the Black Experience in the

United States. He was trying to reconcile the stuff he'd learned with a Christian faith that didn't seem to fit.

Both of your parents had read a couple of Tom Skinner's books, and both were hungry to learn more. Because the way this Skinner guy spoke about the connection between *faith* and *freedom* seemed to call out to something deep inside of them.

Back to the conference. Soul Liberation was up first. The band swayed on the stage, rocking colorful dashikis, and all the members had Afros that stood on top of their heads like fists raised in solidarity. There were twelve thousand college students in the crowd that night, but only about five hundred were Black. And just about all of them had surged to the front of the arena so they would be close to the stage.

As Soul Liberation played, the air in the arena shifted. There were no choir robes or choral hymns. The space filled instead with booming drums and heavy bass, with songs like "Power to the People" and "Put On the Whole Armor." Soon, thousands of White students were on their feet, grooving and swaying and singing along. Every chord and every word seemed to be prepping the crowd for what Skinner would say. His keynote, after all, was titled "The U.S. Racial Crisis and World Evangelism." Which everyone knew. Because it was printed in the Urbana 70 program.

And then there he was. Black suit, white shirt, red tie.

Brown skin.

He began not with platitudes or verses of scripture or words of encouragement. There, in front of five hundred Black students, and *twelve thousand* five hundred White ones, Skinner opened his keynote sermon . . .

. . . with a deep dive into the history of racism.

And your parents spent the next fifty-something minutes having their entire (separate) worlds turned upside down. Skinner reframed their beliefs around a man he called a *radical revolutionary*. A man who he said spoke "to the issue of enslavement" and "injustice" and "inequality." Skinner said that "any gospel that does not want to go to where people are hungry and poverty-stricken and set them free" was *not* the gospel from the holy book your parents looked to for guidance in their lives.

He dropped the proverbial mic with the last line: "The liberator has come!"

The liberator had *come*.

The last line pulsated through the crowd. Students practically leapt out of their seats.

So what does this have to do with you?

Well, it completely shifted your parents' paradigms. Modified their individual missions.

They figured out a way to fit together their faith and their fight for the liberation of Black people. In the two decades prior, the 1950s and 1960s, people like Malcolm X, Fannie Lou Hamer, and Stokely Carmichael—all antiracist—had been confronting segregationists and assimilationists (we'll get to what *those* are shortly). They'd started a movement for Black solidarity, Black cultural pride, and Black economic and political power and agency: the Black Power movement. And once your folks realized they could do *both*—live by and spread the word of the God they'd chosen to worship, *AND* join the fight against racism . . . that those two aims were interrelated?

The rest is history.

Your mom went back to her Christian college and helped start a Black student union that, among other things, challenged racist theology—like racist symbols on dorm room doors and the lack of Black students in extracurricular programming.

And your dad? He went back home, quit the choir at his church, and started organizing programs aimed at challenging other

Christian people to think about the connection between their professed faith and American racism.

One day in 1971, a year after having his world rocked at Urbana 70, your dad attended a class taught by James H. Cone. Cone had written a book called *Black Theology & Black Power* and was known for his teachings on Black liberation theology (aka antiracism + God).

After the class was over, your dad, bold as ever, walked right on up to the professor. (Remember the way he just waltzed onto the basketball court to bring you that college acceptance letter? Yeah, he's been like that for a long time.) "What is your definition of a Christian?" he asked.

Cone's answer was instant: "A Christian is one who is striving for liberation."

And there it was.

A definition.

Which, as *you* will come to see, makes all the difference.

So what's the big deal with the whole definition *thing?* you might be wondering. *Isn't a thing just like . . . whatever it is?*

Well.

As those parents of yours came to discover, having a solid—and agreed-upon—definition of this abstract thing, this *identity* they were trying to embody, gave them concrete goals to pursue. Definitions anchor us in pursuable principles. They give us a jumping-off point for describing the world and our place in it using stable and consistent language so that we're (1) all understanding a thing in the same way, and (2) able to work toward shared stable and consistent goals.

Think about it . . .

When you see a bicycle, you *know* it's a bicycle because *bicycle* has a concrete definition that makes it easily identifiable by . . . well, anyone who knows the concrete definition.

Bicycle: A vehicle with two wheels in tandem with a saddlelike seat and handlebars for steering, usually propelled by pedals connected to the rear wheel with a chain.

Your parents had an agreed-upon definition of *Christian* that they aligned themselves with for the sake of pursuing a common goal: **liberation**. Which we can define as *freedom from incarceration, slavery, or oppressive limitations, including political, social, or economic constraints or racist discrimination, through the elimination of all ideas and policies that create and perpetuate subjugation.*

It has the same goal as antiracism.

So let's define some other things (courtesy of future you).

Racism: A powerful collection of **policies** that sustains **racial inequities or injustices** and is substantiated by ideas of racial hierarchy. Also known as "institutional racism," "structural racism," and "systemic racism."

Racist (adjective): In support of an **inequitable or unjust policy** through action or inaction, or expressing an **idea of racial hierarchy**, both of which produce and normalize **racial inequities or injustices**.

Racist (noun):

NIC'S NOTES:
(That's right. There's no definition here because, as mentioned in the introduction, while this word is frequently utilized as a noun, for our purposes in this book it makes more sense as an adjective. So let's just stick to that here.)

Racial inequity: When two or more racial groups are not standing on relatively equal footing.

Policy: Written and unwritten laws, rules, procedures, processes, regulations, and guidelines that govern people.

Racist policy: Any **policy** that produces or sustains **racial injustice or inequity** between racial groups.

Racist power: Policymakers creating and upholding policies that sustain **racial inequities or injustices**.

Example:
A police department creates a drug-enforcement unit to operate primarily within the predominantly Black and/or Latinx areas. Leads to heavier police presence in areas predominantly populated by Black and/or Latinx people.

Racist idea: Any idea that suggests one racial group is inferior or superior to another racial group in any way.

NIC'S NOTES:
Peep this quote from racist policymaker Thomas Jefferson: "The blacks, whether originally a distinct race, or made distinct by time and circumstances, are inferior to whites in the endowments both of body and mind." Sheesh!

What's more: As *you* exemplified through that MLK-inspired speech full of racist ideas toward the group you belong to, **racist ideas** are learned. Basically, you hear them over and over again from multiple directions until eventually you believe them and accept them into your worldview—oftentimes without even realizing it (or without realizing some of the things you believe are rooted in racist ideas).

But here's the good news: As the title of this book will tell you, there's a whole other way you can (and will) choose to be. A different definable concept you'll latch on to.

Drumroll, pleeeeeease . . .

> **Antiracism:** A powerful collection of **policies** that lead to **racial equity and justice**, and are substantiated by ideas of racial equality.

> **Antiracist (adjective):** Supporting an **equitable and just policy** through action or inaction, or expressing **ideas of racial equality**, both of which produce and normalize **racial equity and justice**.

> **Antiracist (noun):** One who makes the conscious decision to support or enact equitable and just policies, and expresses ideas, that produce and normalize racial equality while denouncing, pointing out, and standing against policies and ideas that sustain racial inequity and injustice.

> **Racial equity:** When two or more racial groups

Example:
Racial equity could look like: relatively equal percentages of home ownership across White, Black, and Latinx families at any given time period; relatively equal life expectancies and infant mortality rates and cancer survivals and diagnoses of chronic diseases and, and, and (you get it) across racial groups.

NIC'S NOTES:
Oh, hi! Just wanted to point out that there's also no such thing as a "race-neutral" policy. Every policy in every institution in every community in every nation is producing or sustaining either <u>racial inequity</u> or <u>racial equity</u>. K, bye.

are standing on relatively equal footing and experience relatively similar and/or equal outcomes.

Antiracist policy: Any **policy** that produces or sustains **racial equity and justice** between racial groups.

Antiracist idea: Any notion that suggests that all racial groups are equals and none need developing.

Example:
No racial group is smarter or less smart than any other racial group; no racial group is more or less violent than any other racial group; no racial group is more or less dangerous than any other racial group; no racial group is more or less studious, athletic, promiscuous, emotionally mature, well-behaved, good at math, physically attractive, and on and on (insert countless other arbitrary characteristics we apply to one another).

In other words, there's hope. And because you now have definitions, you'll (eventually) be able to unearth the **racist** (adjective) stuff both in your mind and out in the world. And you'll be able to counter it with the **antiracist** stuff needed to create and support **antiracist policies**.

With these definitions, we'll literally be able to change the world. Make it a more equitable place.

Final thing to note: There is no neutrality in the racism struggle. **Racist** is not a slur. It doesn't only refer to those who parade around spewing **racist** (adjective) vitriol. When it comes to this fight, we are all either (a) endorsing the notion of a racial hierarchy through our thoughts, actions, or inactions, thereby allowing racial inequities to persevere; or (b) endorsing the idea of racial equality through our thoughts and actions, which involves both *seeing* and *confronting* racial inequities so they can be dismantled. We either perpetuate racism—even through silence—or we choose to oppose it at every opportunity.

With this in mind, be aware: At some point on your journey, you'll be told that the *right* way to deal with racism is to just stop talking about race so much. See people as people and that's that. Zero "color"-consciousness. But this is the thing: A decision to not "see" color—to be "color-blind"—is also a decision to ignore racial inequities . . . which, by default, is a decision to uphold them.

It's important to *see* and *acknowledge* that people look different and are categorized accordingly so you can *see* and *acknowledge* that people are treated differently based on those categories. The goal of **antiracism** isn't to *erase* color differences, but to detach harmful ideas from the colors we see. One either believes problems are rooted in groups of people/characteristics of racial groups or sees the roots of problems in power and policies that uphold racial inequity. We can let racism stand, or we can stand against it.

There's this quote from a powerful antiracist woman named Audre Lorde. She'll say it in 1980—two years before your birth and a decade after your parents have their trajectories shifted at Urbana 70:

> We have *all* been programmed to respond to the human differences between us with fear and loathing and to handle that difference in one of three ways: ignore it, and if that is not possible, copy it if we think it is dominant, or destroy it if we think it is subordinate. But we have no patterns for relating across our human differences as equals.

But *YOU*, my friend, are going to define your terms and choose a different way. Because:

> **Being antiracist (verb):** When one is supporting or enacting policies and expressing ideas that produce and normalize racial equity and equality, or denouncing, pointing out, and standing against policies and ideas that sustain racial inequity and injustice

. . . is and will always be better than:

> **Being racist (verb):** When one is supporting ideas or policies through their action or inaction that produce and normalize racial inequity or injustice, or denouncing and standing against policies and ideas that sustain racial equity and justice.

YOU are going to carry forward an **antiracist** revolution. You just . . . have to actually be born first.

A WORD ABOUT AFFIRMATIVE ACTION—AND OTHER ANTIRACIST POLICIES THAT GET TOSSED INTO THE FAUX CATEGORY OF *REVERSE DISCRIMINATION*

Yes, okay, you want to get on with your story, but we gotta pause to toss in just a *few* more definitions so we can get a solid grip on this **antiracism** thing. It's important.

> **Discrimination:** Treating, considering, or making a distinction in favor of or against a person or people group based on group, class, or category.

When it comes to race, for most of your life you'll be taught that **discrimination** is a bad, bad thing that is inherently **racist**. BUT! What you'll come to realize is that there's a huge difference between **racist discrimination** and **antiracist discrimination**.

> **Racist discrimination:** treating, considering, or making a distinction in favor of or against a person's or people group's race that creates and/or perpetuates racial inequity.

> **Antiracist discrimination:** treating, considering, or making a distinction in favor of or against a person's or people group's race that creates **racial equity**.

Basically, an individual or institution discriminating in a way that keeps inequity going by making sure the dominant racial group keeps most of the wealth and power is *very* different from a person or institution discriminating in a way that *challenges* inequity by assisting and making space for *under*represented racial groups to also acquire wealth and power.

Consider this: A green-haired dad has two kids, one with green hair like his own and the other with blue. Dad gets four donuts, and he gives his green-haired doppelgänger three of them and the blue-haired child just one.

Of course, Blue is like, "Bro, what? We're literally equal in every way but our hair. We should get equal donuts, Pops." And the dad, seeing sense, knows he can't deny that Blue is right. So he's got two options. One: Take one of Green's three donuts and give it to Blue. Boom, equality. Buuuuuut Green isn't with that. For one, Green feels a sense of ownership over all the donuts Green received. And for two, Green secretly feels superior and therefore *deserving* of the extra donuts.

Which leads to option two: The next time Dad gets two donuts, he'll give them *both* to Blue. *Now* things are equal—each kid received three—*and* nothing was taken from Green . . .

Which brings me to Affirmative Action.

In the 1960s—yeaaaaaars before you were born—President Lyndon B. Johnson implemented Affirmative Action (a term coined by John F. Kennedy, by the way). Affirmative Action refers to *sometimes* discriminating in favor of women, people with disabilities, and/or marginalized racial groups in hiring practices with the aim of leveling the employment playing field (creating more *equity*) between White dudes and women, people with disabilities, and people of color as a means of expanding employment opportunities for people of color, people with disabilities, and women.

And this is where folks get real mad and start tossing around the phrase *reverse discrimination**.

The very idea of *any* policy that protects against or remedies the past harm experienced by Americans of color really gets folks in a tizzy . . . even if it's for the sake of creating racial equity. *It's not FAIR,* some say. *EVERYONE should be held to the exact same standard!* It's the equivalent of Green pitching a fit about Blue getting two donuts while Green got none—despite the fact that Blue and Green wind up with an equal number of donuts as a result.

This is the thing, though: Unless EVERYONE is going to be given access to the same resources, holding EVERYONE to the same standard is what's *actually* unfair. Think about it: Say there's a dunk contest. Person A is given a personal trainer, the latest and greatest basketball kicks, and a brand-new professional-grade basketball hoop to practice moves on. But Person B only has videos—watched on a friend's phone when it's available—flip-flops, and a milk crate loosely nailed to a wooden light post.

Would that be a fair competition?

Lyndon B. Johnson said it best in 1965: "You do not take a person who, for years, has been hobbled by chains and liberate him, bring him up to the starting line of a race and then say, 'You are free to compete with all the others,' and still justly believe that you have been completely fair."

Not taking who's receiving the most resources into consideration when it comes to the *competition* that is college admissions creates

*This . . . isn't actually a thing, by the way. Everybody has the ability to discriminate, so discrimination has no direction.

an unfair advantage for the people receiving . . . the most resources.

Oh, you want *evidence* of this idea?

Peep this:

1995: The Regents of the University of California voted to end Affirmative Action programs at all University of California campuses.

1998: Ban goes into effect.

Small sampling of the result: A 36 percent decline in the admission of African American students and a 47 percent decline in the admission of Latinx students.

Oh, 36 or 47 percent isn't *that* much? Okay. How about the *69 percent* drop in Native students and the *60 percent* drop in Black students at UCLA?

Now, the common line of thinking on this is, *"Okay, well, obviously those* 'minorities' *who got in before the Affirmative Action ban weren't as qualified. So banning it* actually *made things fair again because it means spots that should've gone to qualified applicants weren't going to unqualified ones."*

But this is the thing: The "qualification" system doesn't account for widespread racial inequity when it comes to resources. Because not all school systems are created equal. Many of those "qualified" applicants attended private (and distinctly *preparatory*) high schools. Many had tutors when they were struggling and prep classes for standardized tests—which are proven to boost scores by hundreds of points.

Even "qualified" White applicants who *didn't* have access to private schools or tutors or test prep had the advantage of not being stuck behind the bars of racist ideas that impact both their own views of their race and others' views of their race. (Remember how shocked you were about getting into college?)

In order for college admission to truly be fair, a loooooootta factors would have to be taken into consideration . . . the racial wealth gap, inequities in public schooling, stereotype threat, varying measures of performance across educational institutions . . .

Anyway, the point: The only remedy to **racist discrimination** that leads to racial inequity is **antiracist discrimination** that leads to racial equity. To achieve the goal of **racial equity**, **racist discrimination** that created an advantage for White people in the past (and *nobody* can deny that there was a crap-ton of it) will have to be countered with **antiracist discrimination** that levels the playing field for *non*-White people in the present.

As US Supreme Court Justice Harry Blackmun wrote in 1978, "In order to get beyond racism, we must first take account of race. There is no other way. And in order to treat some persons equally, we must treat them differently."

The blue-headed kid needs a couple more donuts for things to really be equal.

- 2 -

OF TWO MINDS: DUELING CONSCIOUSNESS

Okay, back to your story.

So after your parents both had their eyes and ideas blown wide at Urbana 70, they went about their (separate) business with steps full of pep and hearts set on liberation. They both had big ideas for their futures: Ma wanted to hit the mission field. Carry the message of not merely salvation, but *liberation*, through Jesus Christ back to the motherland of Africa. And Dad dreamed of spreading the message creatively by writing liberating poetry.

These were the things on their minds in 1973 when Soul Liberation held a concert in Harlem that turned into a sort of reunion for the New York attendees of Urbana 70. And though it took three years and individual journeys toward the same destination, after *that* show was over, your folks found each other and . . . *Ka-zing!* A spark finally lit.

The timing was a little off: Ma was in full-out pursuit of her dreams and headed to Liberia for nine months. But that obviously didn't stop them (as evidenced by the fact that you were born in 1982).

However, during the years between Ma and Dad connecting and them getting married, things out in the wider world were shifting (again). Because old habits die hard (if at all). And the racist ideas that are as deeply rooted as the ones this country was literally founded on? Well, those are *supremely* difficult to shake.

Take our good friend President Lyndon B. Johnson. Remember him from the previous chapter? The guy who implemented Affirmative Action and made that powerful analogy involving race? Well, what's wild—and is a perfect example of this whole two-minded dueling-consciousness thing we're about to get into—is that while Johnson was saying *that* out one side of his mouth, out the other side he was naming 1965 "the year when this country began a thorough, intelligent, and effective war against crime." Now, this might not sound like *that* big a deal, but as we mentioned, there were a whooole lot of pervasive racist ideas floating around at that point . . . including ones about which demographic was committing the most crime.

Johnson's "war on crime" became President Richard Nixon's War on Drugs in 1971.

And this is where things got *real* interesting.

While there are rumors that Nixon's War on Drugs was racist—in 1994, Nixon's domestic-policy advisor, John Ehrlichman, made some *hefty* allegations about Nixon wanting to use the drug war to "disrupt" the communities he didn't like (Black people and hippies who were antiwar)—the dude who started those rumors spent some time in prison over the scandal* that got Nixon almost impeached.

But.

Even if the War on Drugs Nixon started *wasn't* (completely) rooted in racism, the effects of it *definitely* created an assortment of racial inequities that have yet to be corrected literally half a century later.

This is partially because what Nixon started in 1971,

NIC'S NOTES:
*The Watergate scandal. *Definitely* worth a look, as it led to the first-and only-resignation from presidential office so far.

29

Ronald Reagan doubled down on in 1982. The year you were born.

How? Stronger law enforcement. More police officers. Harsher penalties for consuming or selling drugs. Mandatory sentencing, i.e., a set amount of time required for individuals to be jailed when convicted of specific activities. As a result of these stiffer policies—*not* because there was more law-breaking, mind you—the American prison population *quadrupled* between 1980 and the turn of the millennium.

So? What's the issue? you might be thinking. *If people don't want to go to jail, they shouldn't do illegal things*. Except what emerged as a result of this "stronger law enforcement" didn't make a ton of sense: In 2016, Black and Latinx people wound up *wildly* overrepresented in the incarcerated population—they made up 56 percent of incarcerated people despite being only 31 percent of the overall population—even though drug use rates are about **the same** across Black, Latinx, and White communities.

If you thought the glaring racial inequity in drug arrest numbers compared to drug use statistics was bad, think about what happens when those arrest numbers (the similar-use-rates thing gets totally ignored most of the time) are viewed through the lens of racist ideas. The very nature of said ideas is that they root the statistical disparities in people, not policy. Which means there were some who assumed—also *assume*, since this is still a *Thing* forty years later—that more Black people getting arrested for drug-related activities was *proof* that more Black people used and sold drugs . . . which, by default, *proved* that there's something inherently wrong with Black people.

Interestingly enough, there is *proof* of **policies** that created the racial inequities and keep them chugging along. Like the existence of federal grants that require police to make more drug arrests in order to secure more funding. Despite the similar rates of drug use between White people and Black and Latinx people (yes, I am going to keep repeating that), *and* evidence that White people are more likely to *sell* drugs than Black people, the vast majority of these required arrests happened in low-income areas where drug transactions were more likely to take place out in the open—on street corners, for instance. And due to racial inequities of the socioeconomic type (definitely gonna get to *that* a bit later in your story), said poor areas were full of Black and Latinx people. Combine that with the fact that White Americans had (have!) significantly more political and financial power—which often translates to better legal representation—and you've got the perfect recipe:

Policy-Based Racial Inequities + Racist Ideas = Perpetuation of Racism

And unfortunately, your parents, along with a whoooole bunch of other Black people, bought into the notion that the people—*their* people—were the problem.

They were of two minds. One mind had the fire for liberation . . . but the second got behind incarceration.

PAUSE.

As a reminder, here's how we define the former:

> **Liberation:** freedom from incarceration, slavery, or oppressive limitations, including political, social, or economic constraints or racist discrimination, through the elimination of all ideas and **policies** that create and perpetuate subjugation.

Your parents still wanted that for Black people. The second mind just muddied things a bit. Where on the one hand, Black people *were* calling for the end of police brutality, more jobs, better schools, and drug-treatment programs; on the other, many were also asking for more police officers, tougher and mandatory sentencing, and more jails.

It was like selective empathy. They could see the overt
inequities in policing, employment, education, and rehabilitation on the one side, but did
not pay equal attention to the
socioeconomic factors—read:
poverty—that contributed to
violence in poor areas. If they

NIC'S NOTES:
Restorative = job training,
community building, and the
reallocation of resources into
public schools. Punitive = more
arrests and harsher punishments
as an attempted deterrent
to violence and harm.

did, they may have been able to imagine not having basic necessi-
ties for survival, or the means to acquire them . . . and perhaps they
would've requested restorative measures instead of punitive ones.

Instead, your parents and their contemporaries fell back on that
old racist idea that was the foundation of their ancestors' enslavement: Black people are inferior.

Now, hold up, you're saying. *That's a leap. And quite the accusation.*

That's the trickster nature of dueling consciousness: It can get
so focused on the fruit, it never looks past the branches to the trunk
and the roots. Deep down, your folks were still the people who got
set ablaze at Urbana 70 a dozen years prior—Ma still had that mis-
sionary burning, and Dad had all sorts of poetry crackling inside
him. But "real life" settled in, which is where the two-mindedness
started.

Because the thing about "real life" in the 1980s, especially in the
American middle class—which was (and still is) disproportionately
White—is that there were (largely unspoken) *standards* that had to
be met. Standards wholly and completely set by White people based
on notions of White superiority.

So your folks could no longer look at themselves and other
Black people solely through the eyes of self-determined African
American culture. They had to take on a second set of eyes: those of

the White standard that set all the rules for any sort of advancement.

They developed two minds: one determined to be their full Black selves and liberate Black people through a focus on changes to **racist policy**, the other stuck in the uncomfortable position of trying to fit into White spaces. Which required viewing—and judging—themselves and other Black people through a dirty—aka *racist*—lens.

They wanted to liberate but felt the need to assimilate.

Which brings us to our next set of Very Important Terms. Ready?

> **Segregationist:** One who expresses the **racist** idea that a racial group is permanently inferior and can never be developed, and who supports **policies** that separate that racial group from the perceived superior racial group.

> **Assimilationist:** One who expresses the **racist** idea that a racial group is culturally or behaviorally inferior to the dominant group, and is supporting cultural or behavioral enrichment programs to "develop" that racial group up to the dominant group's standards.

> **Antiracist:** One who expresses the idea that racial groups are equals in every way and that none needs developing, and who supports **policies** that create **racial equity and justice**.

There tended to be two very different battles here. For Black people (and other people of color), including your parents, the internal war/dueling consciousness was between **antiracist** and **assimilationist** ideas. On one side was the **antiracist** belief that Black people were entirely capable of setting their own standards and relying on themselves . . . But on the other side was the **assimilationist** idea that (some) Black people needed to do a better job of meeting the (White) standards for advancement. Pull their pants up. Get off drugs. Stop committing crimes. Go to school. Get off welfare and food stamps.

Correct all the behaviors you condemned in your MLK Day speech. (Oop!)

> **NIC'S NOTES:**
> Fun fact: The demographic with the highest number of individuals receiving government assistance with food and healthcare? White people. This makes perfect sense, considering that White people made up 75.8 percent of the total US population in 2019 . . . but racist stereotypes will have you—and many others—believing most public assistance goes to Black people. #MythBusted

Assimilationist ideas (which do a nasty two-step with **White supremacy**; we'll get to that later) tend to be at the root of both anti-Blackness and internalized racist ideas in communities of color. They are the reason many first-generation Americans aren't taught their immigrant parents' native language and why many people of color alter their natural features to make them appear more European.

This double mind made Black people like your parents feel good by insisting that there was nothing wrong with Black people. But on the flip side, it created a bizarre sense of shame—you'll eventually feel it too—because the double mind also implied that there *was* something wrong with Black *behavior*. Ascribing success to assimilating into White social norms disregards the **policies** behind the conditions that contribute to the "shameful" behaviors of people of all races.

The other battle is a wholly **racist** one: **segregationist** vs. **assimilationist**. Segregationist ideas are rooted in the notion that racial groups are wholly and unchangeably different and that there's a hierarchy based on genetic superiority. White Supremacists fall into this category (obviously), but there are other, more hidden—and therefore insidious—manifestations of this position. Like all-White country clubs. Which will still be a thing when this book is written in 2022.

Less overt but no less destructive are White **assimilationist** ideas. On the one hand, they challenge **segregationist** ideas that people of color are incapable of development and reaching the superior (read: White) standard . . . but on the other is the notion that people of color aren't *permanently* inferior, that they can be *trained* to meet the superior (read: White) standard. Black people and other people of color are viewed like little kids who need to be taught how to act—specifically, how to act more like White people. They are *temporarily* inferior.

This dueling racist consciousness creates two types of **racist policies**: The first is **segregationist policies** aimed at segregating, incarcerating, deporting, and killing people of color. These policies result in things like voter suppression, advancing and unpunished police violence, and increased racial inequities in everything from health outcomes to monetary income.

Example:
Bans on certain ethnic hairstyles or on the use of non-English mother-tongue-languages in certain schools and workplaces.

And then there are **assimilationist policies** and programs. These are aimed at developing, "civilizing," and integrating a racial group based on the (perceived) superior standard.

Thus, your parents—like most Americans, White ones included—

were pulled into a two-minded loop where history and consciousness battled it out:

Black people were told to assimilate, "to acquire the traits held in esteem by the dominant white Americans" → Black people made an attempt at doing just that → It wasn't good/smart/classy/poised/articulate/upstanding/so on and so forth enough because deep down, the belief was that Black people are inherently inferior, so Black people were rejected → Black people decided to do their own thing → Black people doing their own thing were told to assimilate in order to progress.

Around and around they went.

Around and around *you* will go.

But eventually, by being **antiracist**—seeing all racial groups as equal and capable of thriving without needing to develop to meet any one standard—you will be free.

Then you'll help free others by opening *their* eyes to what you see.

And you begin to see very clearly.

- 3 -

POWER
(Aka: The Thing that Makes Race a Thing)

1990.

You're seven years old, going on eight. Rising third grader . . . which involves changing schools, since yours, P.S. 251, doesn't go beyond second.

An interesting fact about that dueling-consciousness thing your parents are inhabiting without realizing: It plays a major role in your educational situation and is therefore a large part of the reason you're visiting a school half an hour away from your home in Queens Village . . . despite there being several within walking distance.

As part of the war between the two minds, many Black people—like your folks—were cool with *living* around other Black people . . . but not so cool with sending their kids—like you—to the nearby public schools. Because those schools were rumored to be *bad,* and the poor Black kids who learned within them were the kind of children two-minded Black folks wanted to keep *their* *good* kids away from.

The results of the duel were already showing up in you: You, Ma, and Dad step up to the front door of Grace Lutheran School—a private school with a majority-Black student body—and are greeted by a Black woman: the school's third-grade teacher.

The school day is long over, so the place is more or less empty and dead quiet. As you make your way up the classroom-lined hall-way behind the teacher, your little eyes lock on the class photos hanging outside of each room. Every single one is full of young faces in varying shades of brown . . . but the sole adult—the teacher—in each picture is White.

And you definitely notice.

Once inside *her* classroom, the one you would inhabit if you wound up at that school the following year, she explains the details of a science experiment that involves raising baby chickens . . . but your seven-year-old wheels are spinning, and you couldn't care less. You all sit down, and your parents get to asking questions: Ma about the curriculum, Dad about the racial makeup of the student body (majority Black, which you already figured based on those pictures you saw, but you tuck the confirmation away).

As the grown-ups talk, you sit, looking around. Trying to imagine students in all the spaces you've seen. Trying to imagine those smiling White faces in the same spaces.

And a realization pops out of your mouth in the form of a question: "Are you the only Black teacher?"

"Yes, but—" she starts to reply.

You cut her off. "Why are you the only Black teacher?"

She shifts her gaze to your parents like it's the most bizarre question she's ever heard. Which confuses you. *You* asked her the question. Why is she looking at *them*?

Ma seems to pick up on something the teacher doesn't say aloud. "He has been reading biographies of Black leaders," she tells the other woman. She's talking about the Junior Black Americans of Achievement books, a critically acclaimed series that you love just as much as your gaming system. They taught you about the long history of harm done to Black people and were the source of *your* budding racial consciousness. "He is very much aware of being Black."

Dad nods, confirming this. And you continue to stare at the teacher, awaiting your answer.

Because at seven years old, you are already waking up to and beginning to take stock of the realities of **racism**.

It—**racism**—feels big. Sasquatch big. King Kong big. Godzilla big. Whole-world-sitting-on-the-shoulders-of-Atlas big. And just as threatening. How could a kid—or even a grown-up—*not* fear being devoured or crushed by it?

What a powerful construction race is.

And I do mean a *construction*. As in a thing that is *built* or *made* out of existing pieces.

We'll get back to second grade shortly, but something funky you'll learn when you're older: **Racism** doesn't actually come from **race**. **Race** comes from **racism**.

Don't believe me? Let's break it down.

First, another definition:

> **Race:** A socially sustained power construct created to separate and define collections of people based on observable shared characteristics.

The wildest part? "Race" is an illusion. There's nothing concrete about it. It's only as real as we believe it to be.

There's a phrase that'll come to prominence when you're in your thirties, and it's mostly used around the concept of "gender": *power construct*. Let's define that too.

> **Power construct:** A concept or idea, created by powerful members of society and perpetuated by large-scale acceptance, that exists not in objective reality but as a result of human interaction.

Race is a **power construct**. And it was created to give credence to some messed-up beliefs and actions held and committed by a people group—"fair"-skinned Europeans—who deemed themselves superior to all others. **"Race"** continues to exist/give and take power/create interpersonal dynamics because a long, long time ago, enough people believed this claim of superiority to make it socially true. Then this *completely unfounded* idea of a human hierarchy based on a *wholly made-up* set of criteria spread across the globe. Unfortunately, with *real* and lasting consequences.

Here's a Mostly Succinct Summary of the Origins of **Race** as a **Power Construct**:

- 1400s: Prince Henry the Navigator of Portugal creates the first transatlantic human-trading policies by using his great wealth to fund Portuguese voyages to West Africa to capture Black bodies for forced labor without pay. Slavery itself wasn't some newfangled thing: Christian and Islamic traders had been enslaving literally any- and everyone for-basically-ever. But the Portuguese shifted the human buying and selling to African bodies exclusively.

- 1450s: Henry's nephew Alfonso—then king—asked this dude named Gomes Eanes de Zurara to write down the story of Henry's African adventures. This is the first transcribed account of perceived Black inferiority. Anybody without white skin was deemed ugly and worthy of enslavement, and the people encountered in Africa were said to have been "lost" (from a Christian perspective), living "like beasts, without any custom of reasonable beings." Thus, separation and hierarchy based on skin tone were created, written down, and subsequently spread around.

- 1500s: Spanish and Portuguese colonizers arrived in what would eventually be called North and South America, and those colonizers lumped all the Indigenous (and brown-skinned) peoples into one group—"Indians" or *negros da terra* (Blacks from the land). Then a dude named Alonso de Zuazo came in and contrasted bodies from Africa, said to be "strong for work," and bodies of the Indigenous peoples, who were said to be "weak" and able to "work only in undemanding tasks." Voilà! Further (completely unfounded) justification for buying and bringing in more "strong" enslaved Africans and killing off the "weak" Indigenous people. Because, you know, there were lands to overtake and money to be made from them.

- 1700s: Our present-day conception of **race** becomes a concretely defined thing thanks to a Swedish dude (with a *terrible* wig, mind you) named Carl Linnaeus. Homie just *decided* to color-code the "races," attach each one to a region of the world, describe their characteristics, and then use these (totally arbitrary!) characteristics to create a bizarre hierarchy:

  » **White:** *Homo sapiens europaeus:* "Vigorous, muscular. Flowing blond hair. Blue eyes. Very smart, inventive. Covered by tight clothing. Ruled by law."
  » **Yellow:** *Homo sapiens asiaticus:* "Melancholy, stern. Black hair; dark eyes. Strict, haughty,

greedy. Covered by loose garments. Ruled by opinion."

» **Red:** *Homo sapiens americanus:* "Ill-tempered, impassive. Thick, straight black hair; wide nostrils; harsh face; beardless. Stubborn, contented, free. Paints himself with red lines. Ruled by custom."

» **Black:** *Homo sapiens afer:* "Sluggish, lazy. Black kinky hair. Silky skin. Flat nose. Thick lips. Females with genital flap and elongated breasts. Crafty, slow, careless. Covered by grease. Ruled by caprice."

So: Christian Prince Henry of Portugal started exclusively trading African bodies (to bypass Muslim traders of enslaved people who traded *all* bodies), thereby making *mad* money for King Alfonso. Money (then, like now) = Power. To justify the fact that they were, you know, buying and selling other human beings, Zurara lumped the darker-skinned peoples from Africa into a single group and then generalized about them in a way that set them apart as inferior. Which then made everybody cool with buying and selling them.

Racist power uses racist (and wholly unfounded) ideas to create, substantiate, and perpetuate racist policies wholly out of self-interest.

And since racist policies need racist ideas to justify them, racist power does everything it can, both overtly (like separate water fountains) and covertly (like heavier policing in lower-income communities predominantly populated by people of color) to keep racism alive.

I know that was a whole lot, but let's get back to you (a person who, even as a kid, was contradicting bad-wig Linnaeus's ideas). The Black third-grade teacher eventually overcomes her surprise at your question about the lack of Black teachers. Though she doesn't actually answer your question.

"Why are you asking that question?" she asks you instead.

"If you have so many Black kids, you should have more Black teachers." (Duh. One plus one equals two, and seven-year-old logic cuts right to the core.)

Long story short, you wind up at a private school closer to home. With a White teacher.

- 4 -

BIOLOGY

You won't remember that teacher's name. She will disappear into the mass of White faces that disturb your peace at some point or another over the course of your life. At times, you will want to blame their Whiteness for their unpleasant behavior: "They said/did (insert racism-rooted slight) because they're White." Or, "You know how White people are." But you'll come to recognize that generalizing the actions of racist White individuals to all White people is just as unhelpful and unjustified as generalizing the individual faults and actions of people of color to entire racial groups.

So, many years into the future, as you embrace **antiracism**, you'll come to view this nameless teacher's actions not through the lens of her Whiteness but as a function of her unchecked racist ideas. Which is important to remember as we get into this thing. You'll understand *why* in the next chapter, but for now, let's talk about what she did.

Third grade. You're in a new school, and your class is mostly Black with a smattering of Asian and Latinx kids. Only three of your classmates are White.

You sit toward the back of the room, near the door, where you can see *everything*. Including all the times Nameless White Teacher ignores raised hands of color and calls on the White kids instead. Or punishes a student of color for doing something one of the White kids got away with.

But none of this seems to bother the other Black kids in your

NIC'S NOTES:
An aside here: This problem isn't specific to your school. Or even to your childhood. Racist ideas have so thoroughly permeated the fabric of our society that in public and private schools through and across time, the preferential treatment of White students by teachers has been a Whole Thing. It's 1990 when you're witnessing this in your third-grade class, but even twenty-eight years later, there will be data that shows Black students are twice as likely as White students to be suspended from public schools.

class. So you don't typically let it bother you . . . but on *this* day, the preferential treatment is so glaring, something snaps inside you.

There's a dark-skinned girl. Smaller and quieter than even you. She sits at the back of the classroom, just like you do, but on the opposite side. The teacher asks a question, and you, noticing everything as per usual, see this girl's hand slowly rise into the air.

Which is a massively huge deal. This is a girl who rarely talks, let alone raises her hand in class. Something has jarred her from her comfort zone, and *you* couldn't be more excited. It makes you smile. A sense of shared triumph over something unspoken.

The teacher looks at the girl—*right* at her—then looks away and instead calls on a White student the moment their hand is in the air. Mind you, the White hand went up *after* the Black girl's. And you *saw* the teacher see her . . .

But now you watch the girl's hand *and* head go down. Taking her spirits with them. And something catches fire inside you. The teacher, of course, doesn't notice your fury or the girl's despondency. She's too busy goo-goo-eyeing one of her White favorites.

The girl's head stays down—which keeps your rage turned up—

through the rest of the class, when you all stand to leave the room, and during the walk to the chapel, where the school has its weekly school-day service. As the service goes on, your blood boils inside every vein.

When the teacher begins motioning your classmates out once the service is over, you don't move. You sit at the edge of the pew and stare her down as she approaches.

"Ibram, time to go," she says pleasantly enough.

You shift your eyes to the cross at the front of the room. "I'm not going anywhere," you reply barely above a whisper.

"What?"

Now you look up at her again. "I'm not going anywhere!" you say, louder this time.

She turns as red as a fire truck. "No!" she says. "You need to leave, right now."

Your classmates are almost out the door, but a handful stop and turn to watch. This just makes her even madder. When she tries again to command you into submission and fails, she reaches out and grabs your shoulder.

Which is a *real* no-go for eight-year-old you. "Don't touch me!" you yell.

She threatens you with a call to the principal. You tell her to go right ahead (in so many words). And as she walks away and a couple of tears break free from your eyes, you think about what you're going to say when this *greater* authority shows up.

When you get older and look back, you'll wonder how differently this teacher would've treated you had you been White. Would she have wondered if you were hurting? Would she have asked you any questions about what might've been going on? You were clearly behaving out of character . . .

But did she even realize that?

You'll wonder if the same racist ideas she displayed in her preferential treatment of the few White students in your class made her attach your resistance to your Blackness. If she automatically categorized it as misbehavior instead of distress. Kids who misbehave aren't seen as worthy of empathy, inquiry, legitimacy, or validation. There are (racist) zero-tolerance policies and no-nonsense approaches to discipline that are disproportionately applied to Black and Brown kids.

NIC'S NOTES:
You know how in professional baseball a batter gets three strikes before he's called out? Well, with zero-tolerance policies, there are *no* strikes—if you break a rule, you receive the maximum punishment, which is often suspension or expulsion, regardless of the circumstances.

With your eight-year-old eyes, though, what you saw was a girl with your same skin color, kinky hair texture, wide nose, and plump lips. A girl who looked and talked the way that you did . . . and who was ignored in favor of kids with skin in varying shades of cream. With straighter hair, lighter eyes, skinnier noses and lips, and a different way of speaking and even dressing.

They seemed a different species of human to you.

But this idea—the notion of genetic biological differences between people of different races—didn't actually come from you. It's a tale as old as (Bible) time. And there's a *very* high likelihood that to your teacher, you and every other student of color in your third-grade class seemed a different species of human than her.

A different and inferior one.

> **Biological racist idea:** Any notion that suggests that the races are meaningfully different in their biology and that these differences create a hierarchy of value.

Biological antiracist idea: Any notion that suggests that the races are the same in their biology and there are no genetic differences that could justify a racial hierarchy.

What makes **biological racist ideas** so insidious—and difficult to weed out—is that the notion of different biologies, of different *forms* of humanity, is low-key the origin of **racist ideas** on the whole. What race-makers "observed" back in the day got attributed to "science" (with *zero* truly scientific foundation, mind you): Black bodies were allegedly stronger for work and could endure more physical strain but were lacking in brain cells, whereas White brains were super advanced and White bodies less suited to the sort of harsh manual labor enslaved peoples were made to endure.

But few people, yourself included up to a point, realize they buy into biological racist ideas. In fact, these ideas are so well-woven into society, you'll find that *most* people believe in some version of biological race distinction. See if any of these sound familiar:

- Black people have "more natural physical ability."
- "Black blood" differs from "White blood."
- "One drop of Negro blood makes a Negro."
- Black people have "certain inherited abilities such as" natural gifts of improvisation, which is "why they predominate in certain fields such as jazz, rap, and basketball,

NIC'S NOTES:
Attached to this idea: Said drop "puts out the light of intellect," according to a man named Thomas Dixon. We all know *this* was a thing people believed for a long time. The "one-drop rule" is STILL a thing people grapple with. Even in 2023, when this book is being published.

and not in other fields, such as classical music, chess, and astronomy."

- Black women have large booties, and Black men have large penises.
- Black people are more sexually driven and therefore more sexually active.

While some of these things might seem harmless—complimentary, even, in a twisted way—the danger of believing in some imaginary biological racial difference lies in **racist power**'s tendency to use said "biological difference" in the justification of inhumanity and **racist policy**. For *centuries*, the so-called Curse of Ham (which was actually placed on Ham's son Canaan but has been used to create distinction between the "races") was plucked out of its context in the Bible's Book of Genesis and used to support the enslavement of dark-skinned African people.

For a while, the concept of polygenesis—the theory that the races are separate species of human with distinct creations—was used to support the idea of biological distinction and therefore hierarchy. And even after this idea of separate biological origins was shut down by scientific principles, the theory Darwin proposed—natural selection, or "survival of the fittest," as his contemporary Herbert Spencer put it—was also eventually taken under the wing of racist power and used to biologically distinguish between and rank the races. The White race was said to be evolving and headed toward perfection, but there were only three possible fates for the "weaker" races: extinction, slavery, or assimilation.

The implications of these perceived biological racial differences will shift over time, and due to the two minds, many people—yourself included—will believe in the idea of genetic differences between the races but attempt to reject the hierarchy... and will fail. (Consider the ideas *you* held about Black kids being less studious.)

But then, in the year 2000, something remarkable happens. After a decade of work and study, researchers from the Human Genome Project release their findings. They are summarized by then–US president Bill Clinton: "[I]n . . . genetic terms, all human beings, regardless of race, are more than 99.9 percent the same."

Were there people who leaned into that remaining 0.1 percent as the explanation for racial—and therefore social and behavioral—differences between people? Absolutely. This was the **segregationist** interpretation of the research. **The assimilationist interpretation** jumped on the notion of "sameness" and tried to use it to eliminate racial categorization and identification altogether—a seemingly well-intentioned strategy, but one that ignored the very real ways race and racism functioned in our world.

But refusing to acknowledge race won't end racism. If we aren't willing to see the existing (and often glaring) inequities between groups of people who, for almost half a millennium, have been classified by **race**, we can't correct these inequities.

To be **antiracist** when it comes to biology is to recognize the 99.9 percent genetic sameness and to focus on ending the racism that's based on the false idea of biological difference.

You don't get in trouble, by the way. After the principal sits down beside you in the chapel (because you don't budge) and hears you out, she agrees to talk to the teacher and then calls Ma. You'll never forget Ma's words to you: "If you are going to protest, then you're going to have to deal with the consequences." No reprimand. No *Don't ever do that again*. Just Ma's liberationist leanings coming to the fore.

No consequences came. The teacher eased up on the students of color and bridled her favoritism. And once third grade ended, you left that school.

But, as you'll soon see, you got lucky.

A WORD ABOUT MICROAGGRESSIONS— WHICH REALLY AREN'T *MICRO* AT ALL

Shortly before your parents hopped on that bus and went to Urbana 70, a Harvard psychiatrist named Chester Pierce was defining a new term: *microaggression*. Pierce, who was African American, used the term to describe the constant verbal and nonverbal slights he witnessed non-Black people inflicting on African Americans. Like a White woman clutching her purse when someone Black is in her proximity. Or referring to a Black person who is being firm as "angry." Or mocking Ebonics and African American Vernacular English for fun. Or following a Black person around a store to *keep an eye on them.*

By the early twenty-first century, the term *microaggression* will be applied more widely and encompass any sort of bias-based degradation of any member of any marginalized group. In the early 2000s, a psychologist named Dr. Derald Wing Sue will further concretely define *microaggressions* as "brief, everyday exchanges that send denigrating messages to certain individuals because of their group membership," and will break the concept down into three more distinct categories: *microassaults*, *microinsults*, and *microinvalidations*.

But as you do your research in the future, you will come to very strongly dislike the term, both as a whole and broken down into its smaller parts: *micro* and *aggression*. You'll come to detest the term's association with a supposedly "post-racial" era that shies away from using the words **racism** and **racist**.

Instead, you'll lean into a different word to describe the persistent daily thrum of slights and jabs aimed at people of color:

~~Microaggressions~~ Racist abuse.

Abuse more accurately describes the actions and their effects on people. Teachers favoring White students over Black ones or doling out harsher punishments to Black students than to White students is abusive. Gaslighting people of color who are justifiably angry over racist jokes is abusive. Suggesting that a Black or Latinx kid only got into college because of Affirmative Action is abusive.

Why?

> **NIC'S NOTES:**
> <u>Gaslighting</u>, which is something you will deal with throughout the course of your life and career, can be defined as "psychological manipulation, frequently over an extended period of time, that causes the victim to question the validity of their own thoughts, feelings, memories, or perception of reality." It typically results in confusion, loss of confidence and self-esteem, and doubts concerning one's own emotional or mental stability. In other words, it's gross.

Because the compounded psychological results of these actions match those of abuse: confusion, distress, anger, worry, depression, anxiety, fatigue, and sometimes suicide.

There's nothing "micro" about any of that.

- 5 -

BEHAVIOR

We're going to jump forward into the future a smidge. Because as we dig into the *inside* work of **being antiracist**, of unpacking deeply rooted racist ideas that involve more abstract concepts, *this* topic—behavior—is paramount.

It winds up becoming the focal point of your MLK Day speech.

1998. By this point, your family has moved to Virginia. You weren't real keen on leaving New York, but we'll get to that later. The most important thing to note *now* is that you're not doing so hot in high school.

The lackluster academic performance began before you left Queens: You more or less checked out during classes and did just enough work to maintain the Cs and Ds required to stay on the basketball team at your old school. And so it continues here in this southern space you now call home.

Unfortunately, it's around this time that the dueling conscious-ness ravaging the brains of the Black adults in your life like some flesh-eating fungus starts to have an impact on *you*. Because while **behavioral racist ideas** were not produced by the Black people in your parents' and grandparents' generations, they swallowed it down like the sweetest (poisoned) honey.

If you remember, we previously discussed how the 1980s saw a rise in drug abuse and addiction *across* racial groups. Fueled by existing **racist ideas**, that correlated with a rise in arrest and incarceration rates—mostly among Black people. We also discussed how **racist power** *has* the power to point to the results of **racist policies**—like heavier policing in low-income areas mostly populated by Black people than in middle- and upper-class areas full of White people where drug use and trafficking numbers are just about the same as in the Black areas—and claim that those results mean something is wrong with the people impacted by said **racist policies**.

It's like pulling the ultimate okey-doke. (This is an old-people term that means "trick" or "scam.") Because codifying behavior as race-based enabled **racist power** to place the blame for policy-based racial inequities on the behavior of the people who were most negatively impacted. And to then link said behavior to entire racial groups.

> **Behavioral racist idea:** Any notion that makes individuals responsible for the perceived behavior of racial groups and makes racial group members responsible for the behavior of individuals.

By the mid-1990s, progressive Americans had more or less abandoned **biological racist ideas** (among a few other iterations of racist ideas we'll get to in the next part of the book). But **behavioral racist ideas** were much harder to shake. In fact, they'll still be kickin' a couple decades into the twenty-FIRST century.

Not that **behavioral racist ideas** are anything new. When you're older, you'll discover that racist power has linked behavior to racial group membership for as long as it's been convenient to do so. Take nineteenth-century, pre–Civil War America. Believe it or not, pro-slavery peeps and abolitionists were in agreement on at least one thing: There were serious flaws in Black behavior. Hypersexuality, immorality, criminality, laziness, poor parenting, idleness, treachery, theft . . . *All* of these were attributed to Black people.

Proslavery theorists attributed these behavioral "deficiencies" to freedom. White mastery—and therefore slavery—was viewed as a civilizing factor. On the flip side, antislavery abolitionists, who were little more than progressive **assimilationists**, attributed the supposed "crippled" intellects, darkened minds, and debased moral natures they saw in Black people to the negative impacts of slavery and oppression.

You'll even see a bit of this latter line of thinking pop back up to society's surface when you're in your early twenties. Dysfunctional and negative traits that are attributed to Black people—such as violence, materialism, colorism, rage, and defeatism—will be associated with the trauma of past slavery and present oppression.

The problem with the proslavery position is pretty evident: It implies that the behavior of Black people as an entity is problematic and can only be *fixed* by the guiding hand of superior (White) people. The other view, though less obviously racist, is just as problematic. The issue isn't that it implies people were negatively affected by slavery. Like, duh, of course they were. It's the suggestion that because they were enslaved—or are descended from enslaved people—Black people on the whole are prone to behave a certain way.

Whatever explanation, or lack thereof, is sitting inside your head in 1998, it can't be denied that a link between "Black behavior*" and *your* behavior—your deeply lackluster scholastic performance—has begun to take root in your mind. How could it not with so many

NIC'S NOTES:
*There's no such thing, by
the way. There is *no* behavior
that can be attributed to an
entire racial group.

(weirdly well-meaning) African American adults publicly harping on the ills of Black youth and using the words of Dr. King to shame the kids of your generation when you behave in ways these two-minded grown folks feel reflect poorly on the entire race?

At sixteen, you feel suffocated by a sense of being judged . . . primarily by older Black people. There's no room for the mistakes of individuals who happen to be Black—yourself included. You not only have to deal with the consequences of your personal decisions and failings, but you have the added weight on your shoulders of feeling like you've let down *everybody* Black. It's a lot.

Ma and Dad don't think this way, thankfully: Instead of looking at your poor performance in school as an indication that you're a part of some doomed and incompetent cohort of 1980s-born Black kids, they see you as *you*—their beloved son Ibram. And they keep trying to push you toward fulfillment of the potential they see in you.

Unfortunately, it doesn't matter much at this point. Because you've already internalized a lot of **behavioral racist ideas** floating through the atmosphere of society like an airborne virus. For instance: As you're entering eleventh grade, your parents encourage you to enroll in International Baccalaureate courses. And despite not having very high expectations of yourself, you bite.

It's a disaster.

Not only do you wind up feeling stranded in a sea full of high-achieving White and Asian students—kids en route to Ivy League universities who compete for the teachers' praise and spend their

Saturdays in SAT test-prep classes—but it also serves to compound both your hatred of school and your not-so-subconscious sense of intellectual inferiority.

What's worse: You internalize your academic struggles as an indication of not only something wrong with you, but with Black people as a whole. Has to be true, right? Wouldn't there be more Black students in your IB classes if you all were smart enough? You have zero doubt that your non-Black classmates see you as an impostor, or worse, the fulfillment of some perceived quota—if they see you at all. It's the same way they, and the teachers, likely look at all Black kids: as less intelligent underachievers.

And how could they not? With faulty data from biased evaluations like the National Assessment of Educational Progress—first administered in 1969—revealing a so-called achievement gap between Black students and basically everyone else in both reading and math, is it any wonder you're convinced everyone in those IB classes thinks you're not smart . . . and you believe them? As far as you know, the standardized tests everyone has to take measure overall intelligence effectively. Which means your White and Asian classmates are genuinely smarter than you.

Right?

Wrong.

Yeah, you read that correctly. In fact, let's spell it out: The idea that your White and Asian classmates are more intelligent than you because they scored better on a test . . . is false.

You'll actually discover this yourself while preparing to apply for graduate school during your senior year of college. There's a test you have to take: the Graduate Record Examination, or GRE. You want to do well, obviously. So you fork over a thousand buck-a-roos (*ouch!*) for a test-prep course that will allegedly boost your score by two hundred points . . . which would be *huge*.

For weeks, you leave your historically Black college and trek over to Florida State University for your course. And as the classes progress, it hits you: This GRE-prep teacher isn't making you smarter. She isn't going over material that will be on the test so you know it inside out, upside down, and backward. She's teaching you test *technique*.

Not the *what* of the test; the *how* to take it effectively.

Which is pretty revealing . . . Why is it that scores on a test purported to measure intellectual ability can be improved by learning better ways of taking it? How accurate can a measure of "intelligence" be if people can do better on it by handing over a little green? *For only one thousand dollars, you too can prove that you're a genius by scoring high on any standardized test!**

Long story short: You spent *years* thinking you weren't intelligent because you didn't do well on standardized tests . . . when all the while, many of the people you were comparing yourself to were learning test-taking techniques that helped them do better. Which means these "standardized" tests—the ones being used to support the idea of an "academic-achievement gap" between the races—aren't actually based on fair and impartial standards.

> *And to think these test scores are weighed heavily in college admissions decisions!

It's like gaslighting to the nth degree.

And it doesn't stop there.

What if I told you that a man who said American intelligence was declining and would "proceed with an accelerating rate as the racial admixture becomes more and more extensive" in 1923 would go on to create a standardized test of his own three years later? And that said test would be used in perpetuity as a measure of so-called "natural ability"?

Even *you* will take it. It was originally called the Scholastic Aptitude Test.

That's right: *the* SAT.

Now, granted, in eleventh-grade IB you're floundering because you're being lazy. You're not putting forth the effort. You don't study much or even pay attention in class. And, frankly, tests make you nervous—largely because you expect to do poorly on them. You expect to do poorly on pretty much *all* things school related. Because you've internalized **racist ideas** (perpetuated by the **racist power** that will center standardized testing as a measure of "intelligence" for decades to come) about Black kids and academic achievement.

It's a struggle now when the results of your individual unstudiousness seem to support the racist ideas in your head about Black behavior, but you'll soon see the light . . .

> **Behavioral antiracist idea:** Any notion that makes racial group behavior fictional and individual behavior real.

Your individual behavior can't reflect on your whole race any more than your race can explain your behavior. This is true of you, the Asian kids in your class (the idea that "Asian kids are good students" is just as absurd as "Black kids don't study"), and even Angela, the cute brown-skinned girl in your twelfth-grade government class who will encourage you to enter that MLK speech contest that is going to change your life . . .

Though it'll take a surprising college encounter with some hardcore behavioral racist ideas—from a fellow Black man—for you to realize it.

6

BLACK
(Aka: The Chapter Where We Start Talking about the N-word)

All right. So we've defined some things, talked about that whole two-minded battle, discussed the role of *power* in race-making, detached biology from the idea of **race**, and acknowledged that racial group membership doesn't predetermine behavioral patterns or incline individuals toward particular actions.

Boom. Mind changed. Eyes and ears opened.

Time to get to the external stuff now, right?

Nope.

Because while you've successfully myth-busted a thing or two, you haven't yet dealt with the impact that those insidious—and deeply conditioned—myths have had on your worldview. So now we gotta get into *your* specific mind and pick some of the uglies apart . . . uglies you don't even realize are in there.

Yet.

The light will flip on inside one of the cluttered rooms of your brain in 2003. At this point, you're not exactly living with an anti-racist mindset when it comes to people of the Caucasian persuasion (we'll get to that in the next chapter). And pretty much everyone in the city of Tallahassee, Florida, knows it. Because you very openly share your ***racist***-by-your-own-future-definition thoughts in a column you write for your college newspaper.

Which, cool. Freedom of speech *and* freedom of the press. You're leaning into them First Amendment rights with verve. Power to the people!

Only problem is that your college newspaper isn't your sole foray into journalism. You're also in the midst of an internship—one you gotta complete to graduate—at a *local* paper: the *Tallahassee Democrat*.

On the fateful day that you begin to open your eyes, you're summoned into the editor's office at the *Democrat*. A tall, light-skinned Black dude, he has some things to say about a piece you wrote in that column of yours at the college paper. He's a smidge uptight. *Pretentious* wouldn't be a stretch. And he seems to take issue with *your* issues with White people.

He critiques. You calmly defend. You know what you believe and why, and you stand firm in it. Yes, at this point, you still see Black people as problematic (which is the main issue here, and more on that in a sec). But the *true* problem, according to your column, is White people and the awful things they do because "they're facing extinction" and "trying to survive."

(You're totally cringing right now, I'm sure.)

You know your ideas about White people are unconventional—perhaps even a hair on the *radical* side—so you are more than ready to support them with what you consider indisputably tenable research. The column had caused a ripple, and White readers had been especially shaken . . . but isn't that the point of good journalism? To reveal the truth and allow it to do whatever work it needs to?

Imagine your surprise when editor man opens his mouth, mentions his "nice car," and then laments about getting pulled over and treated like "one of them n****rs."

Uh-huh. With that *hard R*.

Now, wait, you're thinking. *Didn't you say this dude is* Black? *He clearly doesn't mean it the* real *hard* R *way. He has to be using it the way rappers do.*

Yeah, nah. And you know it.

Dude is totally racist.

While that sinks in, let's pause for a second to run through an exceedingly brief history of the N-word:

- What we know for sure: The version used to *denigrate* (yep, used that term on purpose) Black people here in the United States is derived from the Latin *niger,* the word for "black."
- A version of it—*negars*—was found in the journal of John Rolfe; he used it to reference the first-ever shipment of Africans to Virginia in 1619, and it seemed to be reserved as a title for dark-skinned enslaved people.
- According to the Darwin Correspondence Project, the evolution theorist and his wife were said to have used the term *n****r* as a nickname for Charles in letters they penned to each other in the 1840s; it suggested that "the status of a husband was that of a slave."
- What can't be denied: It's always been a verbal tool to create separation and reinforce notions of hierarchy. If you look it up in the dictionary, one of the definitions says it's "a contemptuous term used to refer to a person of any racial or ethnic origin regarded as contemptible, inferior, ignorant, etc."

No matter how you slice it, the word is undeniably insulting and has been tossed about by people with **racist power** to confer and perpetuate **racist ideas** about the supposed inferiority of

Black people—and non-Black people with dark skin—for a very long time.

So to hear it used in an overtly de*nig*rating way by a fellow Black man—especially one who edits a newspaper and has a certain measure of power over the spread of information—shakes you to your core.

But this isn't an uncommon thing in the 1990s and early 2000s, this idea of certain Black people separating and elevating themselves above other Black people based on some sense of behavioral superiority. There are even Black comedians who lean on these (**racist**) notions in their stand-up routines.

It's the ultimate expression of the dueling consciousness. People like this editor feel an immense amount of **antiracist** pride in Black excellence. To them, high achievers are *proof* that there's nothing inherently wrong with Black people, and they *could* do anything they put their minds to. But on the flip side, there is a sense of **racist** shame in being connected to, and sometimes equated with, "*those* Black people," which is little more than a euphemism for "them n****rs."

Many Black people—yes, including 2003 you—are guilty of perpetuating racist ideas by racializing what they perceive as negative behavior in other Black people. For instance, instead of grouping individual law-breakers who happen to be Black with law-breakers from all racial groups, *criminality* gets attached to "*those* Black people."

But pointing to "them n****rs" as the source of the problem like your editor did just allows **racism** (and **racist policies**) to hide. Even within the minds of Black people. How?

> **Internalized racism:** Subscribing to **ideas** and supporting **policies** that negatively impact one's own racial group and contribute to racial inequities.

On that day, as you look that editor in the face, you come to a powerful realization: You're just like him. And though you'd never use the term he did, in that moment, you can see that every time you say something is wrong with Black people—and back then you said it frequently—you are separating and elevating yourself as superior to "them n****rs."

You are being **racist**.

But Black people can't be racist. They don't have any power.

If you got a dollar for every time someone will say this once you become a prominent proponent of **antiracism**, you'd probably be able to pay off the student loan debt of an entire graduating class at an HBCU.

Thing is: It's not true.

In fact, **racist ideas** are so pervasive and foundational to American life, it would be impossible *not* to be susceptible to them. Anyone can align themselves with **racist power**. *Anyone* can perpetuate **racial inequities** by supporting **racist policies**. Anyone can define an individual by their racial group membership or view an entire racial group through the lens of a single individual.

Anyone.

"(*Insert individual*) got in a car wreck . . . And, I mean, no one is surprised, because we all know (*insert racial group*) can't drive."

"(*Insert racial group*) are terrible drivers, so there's no way I would get in a car with (*insert individual*) behind the wheel."

"(*Insert individual*) really gets around. You know what they say about (*insert racial group*) and their crazy sex drives."

"(*Insert racial group*) are, like, super hypersexual, so (*insert individual*) totally hooked up with that dude she went out with a couple nights ago."

"(*Insert individual*) got caught stealing some dude's phone. It's such a shame that (*insert racial group*) are so prone to lives of crime."

"You know (*insert racial group*) have criminal tendencies. (*Insert individual*) is obviously the person who took (*insert missing thing*)."

All racist.

Okay, fine, but White people have all the institutional *power, so if people of color "subscribe to racist ideas," as you say, it doesn't actually matter because they can't* oppress *anybody.*

Also incorrect. Just ask all of the Black people, Indigenous people, and other individuals of color who have worked their way into positions of authority. I'm sure *they* would take issue with the suggestion that they're "institutionally" powerless. From teachers to doctors to lawyers to store managers to PTA parents to school board members to college deans to K–12 principals to CEOs to journalists to congresspeople to senators to local legislators to mayors to police officers to judges to a whole president AND vice president of the United States.

Black officers have been involved in and responsible for the deaths of unarmed Black civilians *and* have contributed to mass incarceration. Black legislators have passed voting laws that negatively impact—and suppress—Black voters. There are Latinx individuals who are anti-immigration. South Asian individuals who negatively view darker-skinned South Asians. And on and on and on.

The point: *Anyone* can per-petuate **racial inequities** by aligning themselves with **racist power** through unchecked **racist ideas**. Your(Black)self included. Which also means anyone can *challenge** racist power by (1) checking those **racist ideas**, and (2) noticing and pushing back against the **racist policies** said ideas have justified.

Black people—and other people of color—are not powerless, institutionally or otherwise. And it's in recognizing the power you *do* have that you take the next step toward being **antiracist**. Real important stuff here.

Back in the office, you and the editor dude are staring each other down, the **racist** designation he used for certain people in your shared racial group coating the air and making it difficult to breathe. He gives you an ultimatum: Terminate your race column in your college newspaper or be terminated from the internship.

You choose the former—graduating is more important than maintaining a space where you can publicly spew thinly veiled (and racist) vitriol. But it hurts; in shutting down that column, you feel like you're shutting down a part of yourself . . .

And you are. But it's for the best.

You'll see.

ANOTHER (BRIEF) WORD ABOUT THE N-WORD

So now there's an elephant in the room. Because while we discussed the origin and inherent denigratory nature of the N-word with the hard *R*—n****r—we did *not* discuss the other version. The one that hip-hop artists and homies toss around like Frisbees: n***a.

Needless to say, there is and always has been a lot of controversy surrounding the use of n***a by Black and non-Black people alike. But before we get into the weeds of why, let's add a couple definitions to our repertoire, shall we?

> **Slur:** A disparaging remark or slight aimed at a member or members of a particular group, typically used to intimidate and/or remind said group member(s) of their marginalization on a societal level.

There are a *lot* of **slurs**, each specific to some aspect of an individual's humanity that they have little to no control over. There are **slurs** for Black people (like n****r), East Asian people, South Asian people, and Latinx people. There are **slurs** for people of different ethnicities within the same racial group. There are slurs for people who are disabled, people who are neurodivergent, and people who are a part of the LGBTQIAP+ community.

And they're grody. Members of groups deemed "superior" by social norms typically use **slurs** to reinforce their sense of superiority by making others feel small. **Slurs** serve to remind *everyone* of existing hierarchies—whether they're legitimate or not. And their use *now* frequently provokes fear because there are times when slur usage is accompanied by physical violence.*

When editor dude said what he said to you, he was 100 percent using a **slur**.

But there's a twist here.

NIC'S NOTES:
*For some examples of what I mean, read up on lynching during the Jim Crow era. And then read the Matthew Shepard story.

> **Linguistic reappropriation:** The cultural process by which a group reclaims words or language historically used to demean or disparage, creating semantic change that neutralizes the words over time.

Reclaimed slurs are one form of linguistic reappropriation, and *n***a* is a reclaimed slur. They exist in many marginalized communities; you will inevitably hear women and gay men affectionately refer to one another with the B-word (you know . . . the one that actually means "female dog"). Some members of the LGBTQIAP+ community (myself—Nic—included) refer to *themselves* as "queer," which at one point was wholly derogatory.

The thing about reclaimed slurs, though, is there's a significant amount of controversy over who's permitted to use them. Like, are people who are *not* a part of any given marginalized community *allowed* to even speak reclaimed slurs out loud?

Which brings us back to *n***a*.

Once you're out in the world doing the hard work of teaching people about antiracism and why it's important, you're going to encounter a *lot* of White people—teenagers especially—who are very curious about the reclaimed N-word and whether or not they're allowed to use it. A *lot* of them will be asking from a place of discomfort about the idea of being restricted, but some will genuinely wonder if it's racist for *anyone* to use *any* form of the word, Black people included.

The answer: It depends.

Can Black people use the reclaimed N-word in a **racist** way? That is to say, can it be used in a way that ascribes negative traits or behaviors to Black people on the whole? Absolutely.

But it can also be a term of endearment. A statement of solidarity. A reminder of belonging and shared history and experiences.

At the end of the day, no one can truly restrict *anyone's* usage of *any* word. There are non-Black people who would never say "n***a" when there are Black people around but who throw it in the air like confetti when around their non-Black friends. Just like there are people who have no problem using actual **slurs** when not in the company of people who belong to the group they are actively denigrating.

What can be said for sure: *True* **antiracism** can't be for show. Reclaimed slurs are designed to give members of marginalized groups some of their power and agency back. When individuals who are *not* a part of those marginalized groups say or use them, said individuals are reinforcing their *own* societal power, even if it's completely subconscious.

This is the opposite of anti-racism. Think about it: Can someone reinforce their own (unearned) societal power *and* dismantle inequity simultaneously?

Worth a ponder.

NIC'S NOTES:
Reminder: **Racist** vs. **antiracist** is a moment-to-moment thing rooted in deliberate thought and decision-making.

7

WHITE

So now that you know you're *not* powerless and that you *can* absolutely perpetuate inequities that negatively impact you and people like you, let's get into the final almost-pitfall in your pursuit of being antiracist. And be forewarned: You're not going to like what you're about to realize.

NIC'S NOTES:
*No, for real: There was worldwide concern that once the clock struck midnight on January 1, 2000, the world would implode. #Y2K. (Though, fine, hashtags weren't a thing at that point.)

We gotta rewind a little.

It's the year 2000, which you make it into without the world collapsing*, and you're about to begin your freshman year at FAMU—that's Florida A&M University to the uninitiated. Your roommate's name is Clarence, and the two of you couldn't be more different. Clarence, a true southerner, was born and raised in Birmingham, Alabama, and embodies the opposite of your (self-perceived) academic ineptitude; guy's a total whiz kid. His inclination to think critically and analyze *everything* methodically and from multiple angles stands in stark contrast to the untethered theories and ideas you tend to latch on to. Clarence has big goals, a mapped-out life plan, and a sense of clarity that you lack, especially in regard to your sense of self and direction.

As your time together at school wears on, those differences *really* make themselves known in the ways you view and experience the world and the people in it.

Observe: You're standing in the doorway of Clarence's room in your shared apartment a few months into the second semester of your and Clarence's sophomore year. Clarence, knowing you pretty well after almost two years of living together, likely sensed an argument brewing. His cynical pragmatism consistently collided with your dreamy gullibility. He asks you flat-out, "So what you want to tell me?"

You respond, "I think I figured White people out."

Despite it being a rather *bold* assertion, your statement draws not intrigue but head-shaking exasperation from your levelheaded roommate. "What is it now?" he replies.

You don't realize it yet, but your arrival at FAMU is steeped in anti-Black **racist ideas**. In fact, in an essay for English 101, you'll write, "I had never seen so many Black people together with positive motives." (Sheesh!)

However, freshman year is also when you take on some new beliefs—without addressing the existing harmful ones you hold about other members of your own racial group, mind you. They start to take root during the 2000 presidential election. George W. Bush, the Republican elder brother of Florida's governor—Jeb, a conservative White dude who, in the opinions of your FAMU freshman class (among others), has a big blemish on *his* record after deciding to terminate Affirmative Action programs across the state earlier in the year—is running against the sitting vice president, a Democrat. It is your dormmate's and your first time voting in a presidential election, and you've all joined the majority of Black Floridians in voting to save the rest of America from the Bush family.

And things look good. On election night, it's clear that whoever wins Florida will take the whole thing, and shortly after the polls close, Al Gore's face fills the screen on the sole TV in your dorm building's television room, announcing him as the preliminary winner of the state. You go to bed both relieved and triumphant.

Except you wake up the next morning and learn that George W. Bush is holding a *very* narrow lead. And his brother's appointees are overseeing the recount. The conflict of interest seems glaring to you, and for the first time, you get a glimpse into just how unfair things can be.

It's infuriating.

Over the next couple of weeks, you learn that Black people all over the state were prevented from voting for some reason or another: citizens who registered but never received their registration cards; people whose voting locations had been changed without their knowledge; registered voters who were denied a ballot and/or ordered to leave long lines once the polls closed.

Earlier in the year in Florida, fifty-eight thousand people alleged to have felony convictions had been purged from the voting rolls, and though Black people represented only 11 percent of registered voters, they made up 44 percent of the purge list. All in all, close to one hundred and eighty thousand ballots were invalidated in a race won by fewer than six hundred votes.

Initially, two thousand students complete a silent march to the Florida Capitol and conduct a sit-in. But upon returning to campus, still very much enraged, you turn your ire toward the people who look like you—seeking out the nonvoters on campus, shaming them with stories of the individuals who marched and laid their lives down so they *could* vote. You hopped right into a racist power-move as old as time: blaming the victim for their own victimization*.

NIC'S NOTES:
*You're going to see this tactic well into the twenty-first century, especially in regard to police violence committed against people of color.

Slowly but surely, as you watch what looks to you like the complete destruction of democracy as a concept, your gaze shifts away from the deep-rooted and well-hidden belief in *Black people as the problem,* and you lock it onto something new: a passionate and gripping hatred of White people.

The interesting thing here: When you go in search of some sort of evidence to support your hatred, you have zero issue finding it. Just as there are all sorts of pseudoscientific theories and origin stories about the alleged inferiority of Black people, the same sort of concepts exist to explain where White people come from . . . and the source of *their* alleged "devil" nature.

THEORY ONE:

The world was originally all Black, but an evil scientist who was exiled with his followers to a remote island got super pissed and decided to take revenge by creating "upon the earth a devil race." We won't get too into the weeds with details, but long story short, through what was basically colorism-based eugenics, this guy—Yakub was his name—created "these blond, pale-skinned, cold blue-eyed devils."

Eugenics: The practice of "improving" the human species by encouraging people with "good" genes to

73

mate, or stopping people with "bad" genes from mating. (And yes, this is definitely as grody and inhumane as it sounds.)

Way harsh.

From there, Yakub's White people escaped the island and invaded the spaces where Black people lived in peace, turning "what had been a peaceful heaven on earth into a hell torn by quarreling and fighting." Black people locked these White people up in European caves, but then Moses showed up, set them free, and taught them about civilization.

Even if we ignore the fact that *this* Whiteness origin story isn't too far off from a flip of what you learned about where Black people came from—in the African bush, then lifted out and civilized by White enslavers and colonizers, but unsuccessfully, hence the Black descent into criminality and amorality—it's enough not only to hold you in thrall, but to give you an explanation for all the maltreatment you've received from White people across the stretch of your short lifetime.

More important, though, it gave you a hook to hang your hatred cloak on when you thought of all the White lawyers and judges and police officers and state officials and politicians who were involved in what you felt was the decimation of democracy. That did it. It solidified the basic ideas that would carry you into that column you started at your college newspaper: There was something deeply and powerfully wrong with White people, and it made them evil to the core.

THEORY TWO:

The two-cradle theory. Proposed by a Senegalese scholar named Cheikh Anta Diop, *this* theory suggests that the harsh climate and lack of resources in the upper northern hemisphere—aka the northern cradle—created in Europeans barbaric, individualistic, materialistic, and warlike behaviors, which are the source of destruction in the world.

In contrast, the agreeable climate and abundance of resources in the southern cradle catalyzed the African characteristics of community, spirituality, composure, and peace, which are the *true* source of civilization in the world.

Right. It's a lot.

THEORY THREE:

The alleged ruthlessness of the White race is the product of its rearing in the Ice Age. (Cold environment = coldhearted and cold-blooded, perhaps?) And then . . .

THEORY FOUR:

Was proposed by a psychiatrist named Frances Cress Welsing when looking for *biological* evidence: Since White people are the global minority, their "profound sense of numerical inadequacy and color inferiority" causes their "uncontrollable sense of hostility and aggression." The idea here is that survival instincts are what make White people ruthless because they are defending against their own genetic annihilation.

As we saw in the previous chapter, you're eventually made to reckon with the fundamental errors in all of these theories. But through the process of learning and unlearning, you come to realize one very important thing: Hating White people as a collective is not in line with your desire to be antiracist.

Now, this is where things start to get a tad controversial. Because while we've established that *anyone* can subscribe to racist ideas about any racial group of color, once people *really* get to talking about race and racism in the twenty-first century, you'll hear the argument that because **racism** is alllllllll about institutional power and the ability to oppress, Black people and people of color *can't* be **racist** toward White people because Black people and people of color can't oppress or hold White people down on a grand scale.

But once you revisit our definition of a **racist idea**—"Any idea that suggests one racial group is inferior or superior to another racial group in any way"—and also acknowledge that your anti-White thinking both defines individuals by their racial group membership *and* views an entire racial group through the lens of single individuals, it will be difficult to call this hatred of White people as a group anything *but* racist.

In a nutshell, while choosing to be **antiracist** involves standing against and calling out White racism—the racist words spoken, actions taken, and policies enacted by people who are White—it also means choosing *not* to hate White people. There's only something "wrong" with White individuals when they embrace racist ideas and policies . . . and then deny that said ideas and policies are racist. Especially when confronted by people of color.

Have people who are White massacred and enslaved millions of Indigenous and African peoples?

Yes.

Have people who are White colonized and impoverished millions of people of color around the globe while growing rich themselves?

Yes.

Have people who are White produced **racist ideas** to support the **racist policies** that perpetuate **racial inequities** . . . and then blamed the victims?

Absolutely.

Do people who are White but have *not* actively used **racist power**

There's this unfortunate phenomenon where sometimes a White person will get called out for saying or doing something racist by a person of color, and their immediate response is to balk and say that the person of color is being racist for calling out the racism.

Which . . . is racist. How? It deflects from the *truly* racist statement or act and creates a little safety bubble around it, thereby protecting–and therefore perpetuating–the **racism** said statement or act reinforces.

The *antiracist* thing to do here, Dear White Reader who might be on the receiving end of being described as racist, is to resist taking offense, and instead pause to listen, investigate, and reflect. See if said person of color might be correct in their assessment of what was said or done.

to produce **racist policies** still benefit from said policies?

Yup.

But there are no "White genes" to blame for any of this. And none of it has to do with White people being innately evil.

Choosing to be antiracist means not conflating hatred of White racism with hatred of White people. It means seeing individual White people as *individuals* even when they are actively espousing racist ideas. It means never confusing the antiracist hate of racism *from* White people with the racist hate *of* White people.

What you *can* hate with verve?

White supremacy: The belief, theory, or doctrine that White people are inherently superior to people from all other racial and ethnic groups and are therefore rightfully the dominant group in any society.

A WORD (OR TWO) ABOUT WHITENESS

Before being used to label a racial group, the English word *white* referred to the color created by the combined reflection of nearly all the separate wavelengths of either natural or electric light.

Whiteness as applied to members of the racialized people group—typically of European descent and characterized by pale skin tone and very specific facial features—is a power construct (which, as a reminder, is a social structure created by human actions and beliefs that generates power differences between groups).

In conclusion, White people are White for the same reason Black people are Black: because that's what the people who *made* **race**—a hierarchical system of classification for human beings used to justify the barbaric, grossly dehumanizing, and overtly inequitable treatment of specific groupings of people—decided.

That said, there are likely White people who are reading this story of your journey to being antiracist, and learning things that have the potential to make them feel a measure of guilt or discomfort over their Whiteness.

We shall hope that instead of putting the book down during these moments of guilt or discomfort, White readers—who presumably want to be antiracist, as the title of the book suggests—will lean into those uncomfortable feelings and view them as a doorway to empathy.

Because there's no denying that you (and most other Black people and people of color reading this book), through no fault of your own, have at some point—whether consciously, subconsciously, or unconsciously—felt a measure of guilt, shame, or discomfort over your Blackness.

Part Two

OUTSIDE: FACING THE WORLD

I've come to see that the movement from racist to antiracist is always ongoing—it requires understanding and snubbing racism . . . And beyond that, it means standing ready to fight at racism's intersections with other bigotries.

—Dr. Ibram X. Kendi, *How to Be an Antiracist*

- 8 -

COLOR

All right.

So now that you've gotten your mind right regarding *internal* stuff/ideas/paradigms/etc., it's time to flip those eyeballs around and get to connecting some out-there-in-reality dots that'll hopefully reveal a picture of a more equitable world for *all* people.

Let's start by hopping back to that most fateful freshman year of college.

You're at your very first FAMU football game, and your beloved Rattlers are *trouncing* the Morgan State Bears 39-7. You and Clarence are in the stands, watching not only the game but the thick-uniformed, orange-and-green-capped, tall-hatted Marching 100—FAMU's legendary marching band.

And though, thanks to the uniforms, all the band members look alike, you and Clarence look as different as your academic backgrounds and ways of approaching the world.

Where you are deep-brown skinned, Clarence is lighter. And where Clarence's hazel eyes are real, rare though they may be among African Americans, *your* honey-hued irises—or "orange eyes" if you let your friends tell it—are the result of colored contacts you started wearing shortly before coming to FAMU.

The irony here is that you know of other Black people who wear colored contacts . . . but if said contacts are blue or green, you see *those* Black people as straining to look white. You, though? *You* frequently rock cornrows, a hairstyle you *know* is often equated with some racist idea of *thuggery.* In your mind, the lighter eyes are an innocuous enhancement. An innocent means to a slightly more attractive version of yourself.

What you don't realize? The very notion of lighter eyes being "cuter" than your naturally dark ones is rooted in racist ideas about beauty.

Here the dueling consciousness flares again. Because while you love *being* Black, are proud of it even, you're not super keen on *looking* Black. Many of the Black people around you at that time aren't either. And though Whiteness no longer *seems* like it's driving the beauty-standard bus, what has replaced it in this faux "post-racial" world you inhabit in the year 2000 is little more than Eurocentrism in light-skinned blackface.*

Racial ambiguity is (*continues to be*—even in the 21st century) the name of the beauty-pursuit game, but the whole thing is rigged and has been for as long as darker-

*Brief background on blackface: After the Civil War, stage performers used to cover their faces in stuff like shoe polish or greasepaint to make themselves look Black, then create caricatures that perpetuated deeply racist stereotypes about Black people. Though blackface didn't originate in the United States—White actors were painting their faces black to perform Shakespeare's *Othello* in Europe centuries ago—the way it was used here influenced the way White people thought of Black people post-emancipation so much that the most overtly racist, discriminatory laws in US history were named for a blackface minstrel character created by an actor named Thomas Dartmouth Rice: Jim Crow.

skinned people have been deemed inferior—which is basically for *most* of recorded human history. Why?

> **Colorism:** A powerful collection of policies that lead to injustice and inequity between lighter and darker peoples, supported by ideas of racial hierarchy about lighter and darker peoples.

Colorism, a term coined by famed African American writer Alice Walker in 1983, is a tool of **racist power** that perpetuates **racial inequities** in deeply insidious ways. And it's not new. Since time immemorial—read: when Europeans decided that White was synonymous with "civilized and therefore inherently superior"—people with lighter skin (in closer proximity to Whiteness) have been treated differently, and usually better, than people with dark skin.

That whole thing about light-skinned enslaved people typically working in the house whereas dark-skinned people were relegated to the fields? True. Light-skinned people were said to be suited for skilled tasks; dark-skinned individuals were deemed more suitable for work that was physically demanding. Enslavers even *paid* more for light-skinned women than they did for their dark-skinned counterparts. In fact, dark-skinned "field slaves" were said to have bodies that "are, generally, ill-shaped" and hair that was "the farthest removed from the ordinary laws of nature."*

*These appraisals came from theologian and Princeton professor Samuel Stanhope Smith.

What's wild? Even though Light people, historically and presently, tend to receive better treatment than Dark people, racist power has always made ways to keep Light people from receiving the full benefits of Whiteness. Like the racist "one-drop" rule mentioned in Part One of this book.

These color-based **racist ideas** sadly carried over *into* Black people's perceptions of themselves and other Black people. Even after emancipation in 1865, some Light people worked just as hard to distance themselves from Dark people as White people worked to distance themselves from freed Black people.

And this **colorism** thing isn't exclusive to African Americans or even to the United States; inequities between Light and Dark people persist in *every* country touched by European colonialism, from China to India to the Philippines to Brazil.

Colorism is also a source of *intra*racial discrimination: individuals from the same racial or ethnic group discriminating against one another. Which you see firsthand as a freshman at FAMU, where you frequently hear your Black male peers demean, degrade, and dehumanize dark-skinned girls—and guys—in favor of prospects with light skin.

NIC'S NOTES:
I'll never forget being in the Middle East and seeing a commercial on television for a skin-bleaching cream called Fair & Lovely. I also grew up with a friend from India who was *very* intentional about sunscreen application because she did *not* want her skin to get any darker.

Initially, you fall right into stride alongside them—though without realizing it. The first young lady you date at FAMU is lighter than you, with long, straight hair. In fact, your *enlightenment* comes from seeing the way your friends trip all over themselves for her but totally ignore her darker-skinned roommate and best friend. The more awfully they treat the dark-skinned girls, the more you resent *yourself* for liking the light-skinned one.

Which might *seem* like the catalyst for a much-needed course correction . . . but really just gives you a hard shove to the opposite—and, spoiler alert, equally trash—end of the **colorism** spectrum. Not only do you shift to dating *only* dark-skinned girls, but you lift your chin so high, you wind up looking down your own dark nose at those who prefer light-skinned people *and* at light-skinned people themselves.

You wind up joining the age-old ranks of dark-skinned (Black) people who alienate and ostracize light-skinned (Black) people to the point of questioning—and causing *them* to question—whether or not they actually *qualify* as Black.

Yes, on a GRAND scale, the gains of a multicolored race—in employment, education, representation in media, etc.—disproportionately benefit lighter-skinned people. And **racist policies** tend to disproportionately impact those with darker skin.

The real problem with the flip side of pro-light-skin **colorism**—with colorism in general—is that whichever way you spin it, **racist power** still wins. Whether dark-skinned people look down on light-skinned people—which typically stems from resentment over light-skinned people receiving better *overall* treatment due to their closer proximity to Whiteness—or light-skinned people turn their noses up at dark-skinned people, the *real* enemy, unchecked **White supremacy**, gets off scot-free.

So how does one choose to be **antiracist** as it relates to color? Well, as you'll discover, it starts with recognizing that all skin colors—and based on a photography project created by Brazilian artist Angélica Dass, there are at least *four thousand* of them—are good skin colors. That no skin color is any better than any other skin color.

And then the trickier part: Being **antiracist** involves *completely* eliminating any beauty standard that elevates a particular skin or eye color, hair texture, facial feature, or body type shared by any one particular group.

It means diversifying our standards and seeing *all* natural beauty—that's physical appearance without *any* alterations or enhancements—as equal.

Coffee dark or cream light—both are awesome. Almost as awesome as the FAMU Marching 100 during halftime.

But back in middle school—where we're headed next—you certainly haven't realized that yet.

- 9 -

ETHNICITY

Okay, now jumping back six years: all of seventh grade and rolling into eighth. You've left St. Joseph's Parish Day School, the Episcopalian private spot where your parents placed you after that third-grade year with no-name teacher who played (White) favorites. Now you're at a Lutheran school nearby.

But despite said Lutheran school's Christian roots, the way you and your classmates rag on one another is a far cry from "Love thy neighbor as thyself."

There's a dude you call Speedo because he's so uptight. A kid with a small divot in his skull is constantly walloped with camel jokes. A girl with long legs gets mocked for their resemblance to skyscrapers. Overweight kids—of all genders—are mercilessly asked if they're pregnant. And your classmates call *you* Bonk, a reference to a video-game character whose weapon of choice was his overly large head: It made a *bonk bonk bonk* sound as he attacked his enemies. You're on the receiving end of your classmates' insults, and you dish out just as much trash talk as you take. Just like everyone else.

Around this same time, people across the country are glued to televisions and radios, waiting to hear the verdict in what was then a landmark case: that of former college football and NFL superstar O. J. Simpson, a Black man on trial for the murders of his (White) ex-wife and her (White) male friend. And though it'd be difficult for you to explain why, you are deeply invested in this case.

And in your eighth-grade classroom, when the *NOT-GUILTY* verdict is read aloud on the radio, you and your Black classmates leap to your feet, rejoicing and hugging in triumph.

You aren't completely aware of it then, but in the few years prior, deeply unsettling *mis*carriages of justice sent a very clear message: Deliberate harm done to Black bodies doesn't warrant judicial punishment. Rodney King, an African American man, was brutally beaten in Los Angeles. And the perpetrators, a group of police officers, walked free.

This is why the not-guilty verdict in the O. J. Simpson case feels so monumental. To the Black adults around you, and therefore to you and your peers, the results of his trial feel like a tiny nibble of restitution. All the non-Black executors of violence against Black people walked free due to a lack of sufficient evidence of wrongdoing . . . and O. J. Simpson did too.

It's a victory for *all* people who are racialized as Black. Like Abner Louima, a man falsely accused of attacking a police officer and who was then arrested, brutally beaten, and violated in unspeakable ways. Or Amadou Diallo, an unarmed twenty-three-year-old student killed by four plainclothes NYPD officers in a hail of gunfire. Both men were immigrants: Louima from Haiti, and Diallo from Guinea. But that didn't matter. Because no matter where individual Black people are born—whether on US soil or elsewhere—racist violence doesn't differentiate. It just sees *Black.*

You and your seventh- and eighth-grade classmates *DO,* however, differentiate. And there's one kid in your class for whom the "jokes" hit a little different. Because they have less to do with some easy-to-mock personality trait or atypical physical feature—such as a big head like yours—and everything to do with this kid's background. Kwame is his name. And he's Ghanaian.

The taunts and insults aimed at Kwame have a special edge. Doesn't matter in the least that Kwame is the epitome of "cool" at that time: popular, athletic, funny, and good-looking. While in the eyes of your average racist, Kwame would just be *Black*— like O. J., Rodney, Abner, and Amadou—to you and your African American classmates, his Ghanaian background makes him *other*.

Why?

> **Ethnicity:** The sharing of a common and distinctive culture, language, religion, national origin, and/or set of physical features among a group of people.

Kwame isn't *African American,* meaning descended from enslaved people in the United States. He's Ghanaian American, a descendant of people who emigrated from the nation of Ghana in West Africa. And with his specific ethnicity comes specific racist ideas, many of which originate with the trade of enslaved people. So even though you and your classmates are laughing, by spewing these racist ideas in the form of "jokes," you're not only substantiating them, you're dehumanizing other members of the African diaspora—the worldwide collection of people groups descended from native Africans, many of whom were dispersed during the trade of enslaved people.

> **Example:**
> In the United States, the African diaspora includes individuals descended from African people enslaved here or abroad, and those descended from African immigrants.

And you're doing it the same way the traders of enslaved people did. And the same way racist power continues to.

These are **ethnic racist ideas**. And they lead to racist policies that create inequities between racialized ethnic groups. When it

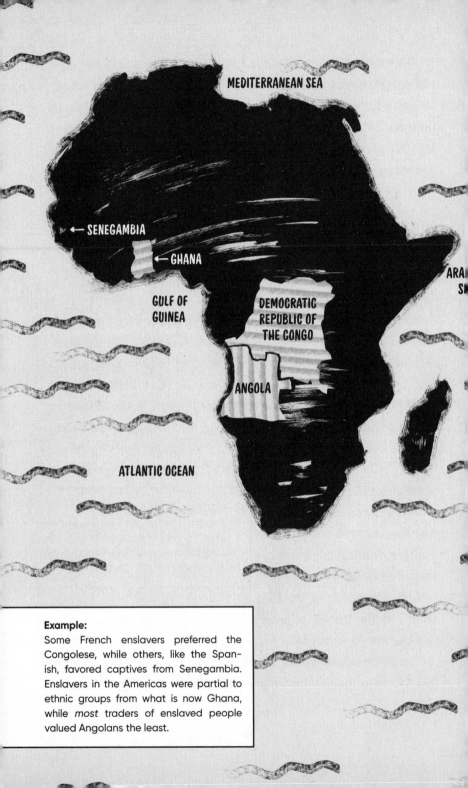

MEDITERRANEAN SEA

← SENEGAMBIA

← GHANA

GULF OF
GUINEA

DEMOCRATIC
REPUBLIC OF
THE CONGO

ANGOLA

ARA
S

ATLANTIC OCEAN

Example:
Some French enslavers preferred the Congolese, while others, like the Spanish, favored captives from Senegambia. Enslavers in the Americas were partial to ethnic groups from what is now Ghana, while *most* traders of enslaved people valued Angolans the least.

comes to Black people, this started back when different enslavers preferred to enslave people from different ethnic groups in different parts of Africa based on their "quality."

And while your and your classmates' "jokes" lean in to hyperbolic notions of Africans being animalistic, barbaric, and uncivilized, the more common and insidious forms of **ethnic racist ideas** turn members of the same racialized groups against one another. Which, like with colorism, lets **racist power** off the hook.

And **ethnic racism** isn't new, nor is it confined to Black people. Between the 1880s and 1960s, a number of federal acts were put in place to limit non-European immigration to the United States. The Chinese Exclusion Act of 1882 was expanded in 1917, creating an "Asiatic Barred Zone" to limit East Asian immigrants; the Emergency Quota Act of 1921 and the Immigration Act of 1924 limited immigrants from Africa, Eastern and Southern Europe, *and* Asia.

And all to make way for more immigrants from Scandinavia, the British Isles, and Germany . . . *White* immigrants. Because in the early twentieth century, ethnic groups racialized as White—which was (and is) determined in large part by skin tone, hair texture, and certain other physical features—were considered superior to all other racialized ethnic groups.

Unfortunately, you'll discover that despite major antiracist strides between the 1960s and early 2000s, notions of White superiority and racist ideas about what makes a person "American" persist into the twenty-first century . . . and are said to be "good for America."

Senator Jeff Sessions said precisely that when explaining why he felt the US government should do something to slow the growth of the non-US-born population. Citing (racist) policies put in place in the 1920s that did, in fact, slow immigration, Sessions also suggested that assimilation "created really the solid middle class of America." He carried these ideas into his role as attorney general, a position he held from 2017 to 2018. Anti-Latinx, anti–Middle Eastern, and anti-Black immigration policies enacted during this period were a frightening throwback to the racist legislation from a century prior, which serves as a vivid reminder that to **racist power**, even if there *is* a sense of hierarchy regarding different ethnic groups—e.g., African, Cuban, and East Asian immigrants being viewed more favorably than African American, Mexican, and South Asian peoples—the goal is to maintain racist ideas of inferiority and to perpetuate racial inequities.

This is why it's vital to both recognize and resist ethnic racist ideas, both in our own racial group and with regard to other racial groups. People of Chinese or Korean descent are not "naturally" better/smarter/more attractive than people of Indian or Pakistani descent—and all are racialized as "Asian." People of Nigerian or Ghanaian descent are not "naturally" more studious/industrious/ambitious than people of African American or Jamaican descent—and all are racialized as "Black." People of Venezuelan or Cuban descent are not "naturally" more honest/intelligent/prosperous than people of Mexican or Salvadoran descent—and all are racialized as "Latinx."

Choosing **to be antiracist** means viewing *all* ethnic groups within *all* race categories as equals in *all* their differences. It means shutting down all conceptions of ethnic hierarchies when they arise (and they *will* arise) and not only pushing back at the racist ideas about one's own ethnic group, but also refusing to consume and regurgitate racist ideas about other ethnic groups.

It means focusing on the **policies** that create inequities between racialized ethnic groups and not on the ethnic groups themselves.

You haven't learned that yet, though. And you won't have learned it by the end of eighth grade. You—and your classmates—will continue to clown Kwame over his African heritage, and for what it's worth, Kwame dishes it right back.

But a change is coming: You, my friend, are headed to high school.

A WORD ABOUT
THE TRAITOROUS-CHIEFTAIN MYTH

You'll hear it a thousand jillion times from other African Americans as justification for their ethnic racist ideas toward diasporic Africans: *Man, I don't rock with Africans. They sold us down the river!*

The idea here is that the transatlantic trade of enslaved people was supplied by African chiefs who were selling their *own* people to Europeans. It is *the* ultimate act of treachery.

At least . . . it would be if it were true.

The reality: What we now think of as **ethnicity** existed long before Europeans came up with the concept of **race** and lumped a whooooooole lot of diverse ethnic groups together based on continent of origin and physical features—like skin tone. So in various places, Africa included, people were grouped by superficial common traits. In other words, just because Europeans looked at "Africans" through the (wholly made-up) lens of **race**—and therefore monolithically*—doesn't mean alllllllll the separate African ethnic groups were suddenly like, "OMG, y'all, we are *totally* one people now!" So while, yes, there were "Africans" selling other "Africans," to put it in monolithic (and racist) terms, it wasn't *treachery* in the way that we think of *that* term, because the sellers typically weren't selling mem-

*Which—spoiler alert—is not only racist, but also how race as a concept got rolling.

bers of their own ethnic groups. They were selling members of *other* ethnic groups.

Think about it like this: Citizens of various European countries aren't all loyal to one another and *"We are all one people!"* just because they originated on the same continent. France and Germany, despite having a shared border, were on opposite sides during World War II. In fact, what people tend to remember most about World War II is the result of nasty propaganda about a specific group: Jewish people. *European* Jewish people, to be exact. Who were, based on the original conception of race, just as White as the countrymen—be they German, Italian, Austrian, Soviet, etc.—who were committing all sorts of atrocities against said Jewish people.

Is it disgustingly barbaric and inhumane for human beings to sell other human beings? Absolutely. The point here is that an individual on the continent of Africa from ethnic group A who sold an individual on the continent of Africa from ethnic group B to a trader of enslaved people didn't think of the ethnic group B person as "their own people" any more than a French or British person would've considered a German or Italian person "their own people" during World War II.

NIC'S NOTES:
Okay, but what about Australia? People say "Australians" all the time. Are *they* being racist? Well, it depends on who you ask—because political geography changes all the time. The continent of Australia is actually made up of three islands, one and a half of which are independent countries: Australia, Tasmania (an island state of Australia), and New Guinea. And ain't nobody out here calling the people of Tasmania or New Guinea "Australians."

Or even now.

Because lumping allllllll the people on a continent made up of different nations into a single group—which seems to happen pretty frequently with Africa—is . . .

(Wait for it . . .)

(Almost theeeeeere . . .)

Yep.

You guessed it: **racist**.

- 10 -

BODY

Ninth grade.

Not only do you wash your hands of wearing uniforms and attending mandatory in-school religious services—*Chapel*, if you're feeling fancy—but you leave the private-school world altogether in favor of a public high school called John Bowne in Flushing, Queens, near the Long Island Expressway. Your Haitian neighbor Gil goes there too.

Interestingly enough, the area due south of John Bowne looked totally different when Dad was a kid there. In the mid-1950s, your grandmother was permitted to move into the Pomonok Houses, which in that era were predominantly White . . . to the point where, throughout his local elementary schooling, Dad never saw a single other Black student.

The area doesn't look like that now, though; by 1996, the majority of the White people had left for suburban Long Island, a result of a fascinating (**racist**) phenomenon known as *White flight*—the large-scale migration of White people out of areas that are becoming more racially diverse.

In ninth grade, both your school and your school's neighborhood are diverse and predominantly populated by people of color. John Bowne is a dazzling sea of varying ethnicities, most of which are racialized as Black, Latinx, or Asian. A veritable wonderland of cultures.

But you don't experience it that way. Because as your body begins to change (yay, puberty!), you become increasingly, though subconsciously, aware of the fact that all around you, people are afraid of it.

Yourself included.

> **Bodily racist idea:** Any notion that a group of racialized bodies is more animallike and violent than others.

While the origins of **bodily racist ideas** are no mystery—honestly, this is one of the cases in which the notion of **race** was created to justify messed-up ideas about people who lived in brown- and dark-skinned bodies—it remains one of the most deeply entrenched and difficult-to-shake manifestations of **racist ideas**. In 1995, on the same day as the world-famous Million Man March*, President Bill Clinton gave a speech at the University of Texas that encapsulated a very specific flavor of fear, one born of **bodily racist ideas.**

"Blacks must understand and acknowledge the roots of White fear in America," Clinton said. "There is a legitimate fear of the violence that is too prevalent in our urban areas . . . By experience or at least what people see on the news at night, violence for . . . White people too often has a Black face."

What's wild is that even though this fear *seems* to be legitimate and substantiated by data (it's not, but we'll get to that shortly), the ideas the fear came from preceded any sort of evidence. Even when

Black people were *enslaved*—wholly under the thumb of enslavers who kept them in line with all sorts of brutality—they were viewed as "creatures" and "ruthless savages." Post-emancipation, when Black people were trying to find their bearings and very much afraid of *White* people and the terror they wrought on Black bodies with abandon, the *Black* person—or "poor African," according to Senator Benjamin Tillman in 1903—was deemed "a wild beast seeking whom he may devour."

It was the epitome of **racist** propaganda. And it has revealed itself over the course of history as justification for lynchings, segregation, deportation, and mass incarceration.

Unfortunately, these ideas endure. Though you aren't likely to hear anyone use *beast* or *savage* in reference to the Black body in the twenty-first century (not even a person who believes that wants the smoke that would come with saying it aloud now), notions of the Black body as inherently violent—of Black people as "dangerous"—persist.

In ninth grade, even you buy into them. Most Black people, even the ones who *do* choose to act violently (which has nothing to do with them being Black), are susceptible to this particular racist idea.

It's **bodily racist ideas** that make your parents fear for your life when you're walking around your own Black neighborhood, and bodily racist ideas that keep you on high alert and make you afraid of bumping into or making eye contact with your Black classmates. **Bodily racist ideas** are what cause people to clutch their belongings when Black people, and especially Black males, step onto an elevator. **Bodily racist ideas** are also at the root of many tragic Black deaths at the hands of both civilians and police officers: Trayvon Martin, Tamir Rice, Jordan Davis, Atatiana Jefferson, Elijah McClain, Michael Brown, Breonna Taylor, Freddie Gray, Philando Castile, Ahmaud Arbery, Rayshard Brooks,

Ma'Khia Bryant, and George Floyd, just to name a few (and there are *many* others).

And **bodily racist ideas** were the foundation for the now-infamous super-predator myth that swept over the country in late 1995 and led to drastic changes in youth punishment policies that, as of the early 2020s, *still* disproportionately impact Black and Brown teenagers and often lead to long stretches of incarceration that begin before some kids are even old enough to get a driver's license.

Does it matter that the siren sounded by Princeton political scientist John J. DiIulio Jr. was a false alarm? That the drastic increases in violence committed by kids in "Black inner-city neighborhoods" never happened? That there was actually a *decrease* in the sort of violence he *warned* everybody about?

Not really. Because many of the things DiIulio and his eventual co-authors said have yet to unstick from the American psyche:

"Most inner-city children grow up surrounded by teenagers and adults who are themselves deviant, delinquent, or criminal."

"A new generation of street criminals is upon us—the youngest, biggest, and baddest generation any society had ever known."

"[R]adically impulsive, brutally remorseless youngsters, including ever more preteenage boys who murder, assault, rape, rob, burglarize, deal deadly drugs, join gun-toting gangs, and create communal disorders."

Sounds awful, right? Never mind that the scary swarm of super predators never showed up. By the late 1990s, violence had begun to decline (dramatically) and homicides were at their lowest rate since the 1980s.

Which . . . didn't actually matter. Because "tough on crime" policies have never correlated with actual harm. In fact, most race-related fear—especially of Black, Latinx, Asian, and Middle Eastern people—is wildly disproportionate to actual violence carried out by individuals from these backgrounds. The patriotic White dude strolling around a protest with an assault rifle is just exercising his Second Amendment rights . . . but the Brown or Black body kneeling in prayer to Allah or the Black body walking with a hood on and a pack of Skittles in hand or the East Asian body running their business during a global pandemic? *Those* bodies are the truly threatening ones.

The problem is, because these (**racist**) ideas are so deeply embedded, when an *individual* Black, Latinx, or Middle Eastern person *does* choose to act violently, said action serves as a form of **confirmation bias**.

> **Confirmation bias:** The tendency to interpret, recall, or search for information in a way that supports one's existing beliefs.

You had a series of frightening firsthand experiences with this in eighth grade. Like your involvement in what we'll call a *crew collision*: when the (informal) group of guys you ran with happened upon another crew, and hard stares turned to insults turned to threats turned to flying fists. It left you aware of the physical harm you're capable of inflicting on another person and scared of not only what other Black bodies might do to you, but what cops might do to your Black body.

As a freshman in high school, you also have frequent encounters with a kid everyone calls Smurf, and his way of moving through the world falls right in line with the mythical "super predator." Like the time he points a gun at you while you're on your way home from school on the public bus. More or less to test your mettle. See if you'll flinch. (You pass.) And another time, you watch as Smurf and his crew jump an unsuspecting South Asian kid, take his Walkman*, and flee, leaving one member of said

NIC'S NOTES:
*A Walkman is the electronic device dinosaurs used to listen to music on with headphones; also known as the great-grandfather of music streaming via smartphone.

crew behind to see if anyone would help the guy.

But here's the thing: Even in your neighborhood, where you are surrounded by other Black bodies, there are far more days when no one harms, threatens, or bothers you than days when someone does. And there are more hugs and dances and good times than swinging fists, firing guns, and early deaths.

Except no one, yourself included, thinks of things that way. Since, statistically speaking, there *are* more recorded instances of violent harm in "urban" majority-Black neighborhoods, most people unknowingly lean into **bodily racist ideas** and connect Blackness to criminality. Reinforcing the fear of the Black body.

What gets missed: *Urban* is often used as a euphemism for "low-income." And if we shift the slightest bit and look at the relationship between low-income/high-unemployment rates and levels of violence in *any* area, be it majority Black, Latinx, or otherwise, there's a pretty high correlation. It's true in majority-White neighborhoods too.

What this means: If more people were willing to pull back from their **bodily racist ideas**–based zoom lens, they'd be able to see and admit that violence has nothing to do with Blackness and everything to do with poverty. Poor and unemployed Latinx and White people are statistically just as prone to making law-breaking decisions as poor Black people. Not because they're Latinx, White, or Black or poor . . . but because of the impoverished conditions they live in, where *many* of the things they do to survive are criminalized.

Bodily antiracist ideas do away with the (**racist**) idea that cer-

NIC'S NOTES:
FYI: Rates of violence
tend to be far lower in
middle- and upper-income
majority-Black neighborhoods
than in low-income White
neighborhoods. More evidence
that violence has more to do
with poverty than Blackness.

tain bodies—especially Black ones—are dangerous by virtue of their existence. It means not viewing relatively high rates of recorded violence in low-income Black neighborhoods as confirmation or evidence that Black people are innately more violent.

Choosing to be antiracist means humanizing, deracializing, and individualizing both violent *and* nonviolent behavior. Yes, Smurf is Black, and he does terrible, harmful things . . . but you and a decent chunk of your John Bowne classmates are also Black, and you do not.

Let's also not forget that the *vast* majority of domestic terror attacks and/or mass shootings in the United States are carried out by White people. That the violence unleashed on enslaved Black people was at the hands of White people. If these behaviors can be individualized, so can those of Black people.

And besides, **racist policies** put in place by **racist power** are a form of low-lying violence all their own.

- 11 -

GENDER

So. Before we go any further, this is the part where I, the fabulous narrator of your (nonlinear) life's journey to becoming antiracist, have decided to break the fourth wall and introduce myself for real. Because these next couple of chapters in particular are hyper relevant to *my* existence. Despite what totally sounds like the moniker of a White fraternity bro, I, Nic Stone, am a queer Black woman. (Surprise!)

The lessons you're about to learn from a queer Black woman—and an antiracist one at that—validate many of *my* experiences moving through the sexist, racist, and queerphobic world we inhabit. And you getting a solid grip on said discoveries makes life a smidge easier for *me*.

So let's get into it.

First, a clarification before we move forward: What we think of as "gender" only exists because somebody at some point long, long ago decided that any person—or any animal, really—could be placed in one of two categories depending on the visible reproductive organs they were born with.

*For the most part is very important here because there are also people who have some or all parts of both reproductive organ sets and therefore *can't* be shoved into a traditional gender box. They are referred to as *intersex*.

Because, for the *most* part*, only two different kinds showed up. Penis and testicles = one category ("male"). Vagina = other category ("female").

Over time, as other characteristics were observed in multiple members of each category, said characteristics got added to what came to mind when people thought of the terms *male* and *female*. Everyone agreed, those ideas got passed down and passed down, and boom: The concepts were accepted and perpetuated as hard-and-fast *truth* . . .

But it's a truth that'll only *stay* true if people decide to keep believing that one set of reproductive parts means "male" and the other means "female."

Fortunately, you become a person who shifts away from that traditional belief.

Fast-forward. Like, *way* forward. Like, a decade or so forward from your gat-strapped Smurf encounter/brush with death on a public bus. You're now in graduate school at Temple University in pursuit of an advanced degree in African American studies. There you meet two Black women who more or less shatter and then rebuild your conceptions of Black women *and* Black womanhood, which then broadens your understanding of the way race interacts with other identity factors in the lives of racialized individuals.

Kaila is tall, solid-framed, and consistently made-up. She is also a self-proclaimed feminist and a lesbian, but what impacts you most about Kaila is her refusal to shrink or hide. She shoots straight. Doesn't self-censor. Won't bend or contort into unnatural shapes for the sake of meeting expectations, fitting into a box, or avoiding judgment and/or ridicule. She is unapologetically precisely who she is at all times and under all circumstances.

Yaba is Kaila's bestie, and together they are an unstoppable force. When you think of the word *Black* as a cultural and expressive concept, Yaba is who comes to mind. A woman of Ghanaian descent—who you know *not* to clown the way you used to clown Kwame in middle school—with a southern flair from her upbringing in New Orleans, Yaba is a great example of harmony between African and African American. She has a wealth of knowledge about—and respect for—both the continent of Africa and the African diaspora. Yaba is the most ethnically antiracist person you've ever met.

The combined strength of these two women who, by virtue of the way they move and speak, *clearly* reject any notion of female diminution—which is the act, process, or instance of becoming less in size or importance—makes *you* feel small and ignorant. This is in part because the very existence of women like them catches you off guard . . . especially since you *start* grad school as a racist sexist.

Of note: This isn't your fault. You, like most people—myself included—with ways of thinking that keep the wheels of oppression spinning? Young people are products of our environment. Because as you'll learn, the status quo—the existing societal structure regarding social or political issues—is a very real thing. And unless we pause to examine it and then challenge its flaws, it rolls on, thriving on our ignorance and silence.

This is *especially* true of intersectional bias.

> **Intersectionality:** The interconnected nature of social categorizations—race, gender, class, orientation, dis/ability, ethnicity—as they apply to any given individual or group, creating the experience of overlapping systems of oppression.

Take, for example, one of the women mentioned previously, Kaila. As a queer Black woman, she gets hit with the triple whammy of homophobia, racism, *and* sexism in a myriad of combinations and often all at once.

But back to you. When you meet Kaila and Yaba, you've yet to even realize the biases you wear like a 1990s Starter jacket. The scariest part is that no one had to *teach* you to be racist or sexist. Because in the world you inhabit, those dispositions are the default; you weren't raised to NOT be those things, so there you have it.

This is one of the great dangers of *not* deliberately pursuing antiracism. Saying and/or doing nothing allows *multiple* systems of oppression to thrive. You arrive at Temple as a racist Black patriarchist solely because you weren't raised to be an antiracist Black feminist.

But an antiracist Black feminist you will become. Because Kaila and Yaba open your eyes to something new: **gender racism**.

Uhhh, whut?

Right. Let's define a couple more things:

Race-gender: The single identity marker created by combining an individual or group's race and gender identity.

Example:
"Black woman," "White men," "Latinx trans woman," "Asian nonbinary people"

Gender racist idea: Any notion that suggests that one race-gender is superior or inferior to another race-gender in any way, or justifies policies that lead to injustice or inequity between race-genders.

Initially, your notions of gender match Ma's and Dad's. And *their* ideas, though sometimes unconventional, were

Example:
Unlike a lot of men in his generation, Dad rejected the idea that masculine strength was a function of some warped notion of feminine weakness.

partially reflective of their (sexist) religious beliefs. Beliefs based on teachings that factored heavily in the development of an American status quo when it comes to gender.

The basics of this status quo:

- An individual's **gender** is fixed and determined by their chromosomes and reproductive organs: XX = vagina, uterus, ovaries = **female**; XY = penis, testes, prostate = **male**.
- Males are bigger/stronger and are meant to be dominant and to lead/protect/provide.
- Females are smaller/weaker and are meant to be submissive and to follow. And, you know, make babies and raise them to fit the aforementioned prototypes.

Throughout the course of recorded history, *any* deviation from these three points has carried significant social consequences. So when one combines these gender norms with racist ideas . . . well, things can get a little depressing.

Take Black women for instance. Racism creates a hierarchy of the races, and sexism a hierarchy of the sexes. Which means that in integrated women's spaces, Black women have to contend with racism. And on the flip side, in coed Black spaces, Black women are faced with sexism. Don't even get me started on integrated coed spaces.

The same is true for most women of color: racism in female spaces, sexism in coed unicultural spaces. So in integrated coed spaces, women of color are subjected to both.

Gender racism is at the root of some alarming race-gender inequities:

NIC'S NOTES:
Of note: The race-gender
with the highest average
income in the United States
as of early 2022 was Asian
men. And the lowest? Latinx
women.

- Black women with some college education make just $29 more per week than White women with high school degrees, *and* Black women have to earn graduate degrees in order to earn as much as or more than White women with bachelor's degrees.
- Black and Native women experience poverty at a higher rate than *any* other race-gender groups.
- Black women are three times more likely to die from pregnancy-related causes than White women are.
- Black girls are over three times more likely to be incarcerated than their White peers.
- The birth rate among Black and Latina teens is more than double that of White teens.

I saved those final two for last on purpose. Because most people who hear those statistics would *immediately* pipe up with something along the lines of "Well, Black girls are 'harder' and therefore more likely to commit crimes," and/or "Black girls and Latinas are more promiscuous." Neither of which has ever been proven true. *This* is **gender racism** at its finest: It ignores external and policy-based factors that contribute to race-gender inequities—like poverty, for instance (. . . and considering that, on average, Black and Latina women earn $0.64 and $0.57 respectively for every $1.00 paid to White men with *the exact same credentials*, is it any wonder Black and Latina women experience some of the highest rates of poverty in this country?)—and it shoves the source of the inequities onto the shoulders of race-gender groups.

In addition to sexist ideas, **gender racist ideas** also negatively impact White women and girls. Because of the combined ideas that (1) "real" women are weak, chaste, submissive, and in need of rescue by men (sexist ideas), and (2) White is supreme (racist idea), the epitome of femininity—and therefore "womanhood"—is presumed to be the weak White damsel in distress. Which means strong White women who take ownership of their bodies and who are financially independent are often considered unlikeable, overbearing, and even "bitchy," and are frequently prevented from professional advancement. (Ever heard of Hillary Clinton?)

And on the flip side, in addition to regular ol' racism, **gender racist ideas** also negatively impact Black men and men of color. Sexist ideas say real men are strong, stoic, and able to withstand more than women; racist ideas say White is civilized and supreme. Put them together, and you get a whole mess of gender racist ideas. Men (strong) + Black (violent and uncivilized) = Black men are dangerous; men (strong) + Asian (passive and submissive) = Asian men are weak, and therefore not truly men; men (strong) + Latinx (amoral and hypersexual) = Latino men are rapists.

On and on it goes.

But there's a solution (obviously . . . it's why we're talking about it).

The more you get to know Kaila and Yaba, the more you'll see that they embody a powerful principle from the Combahee River Collective Statement, written in 1977 by Barbara Smith, Demita Frazier, and Beverly Smith, a trio of antiracist Black feminists. They didn't want Black women—or any other people group, for that matter—to be viewed as inferior or superior to any other group. Their antiracist belief is one that you'll eventually latch on to: "To be recognized as human, levelly human, is enough."

- 12 -

ORIENTATION

In addition to the understanding of race-gender you first encounter in grad school, Kaila and Yaba—as well as a couple of other new friends, Weckea and Monica—also introduce you to another important identity intersection you need to get your head around in your pursuit of being antiracist: that of the race-orientation.

> **Race-orientation:** The single identity marker created by combining racial group membership and sexual or romantic orientation.
>
> **Example:**
> Kaila is a Black lesbian.

(*Of note: Race-orientations can be tricky to define because orientation terms, which are often thought of as labels, are . . . tricky to define. The *point* of this chapter will be clear as you read on, but this is a good spot to point out that (1) words are limited when it comes to the fullness of being human, and (2) with those limitations come limits on the ability to agree upon definitions. K, moving on.*)

Initially, your eyes are forced open when another friend we'll call R outs Weckea to you while you and R are eating lunch together one day. "You know Weckea is gay, right?" she says, totally unprompted.

You did *not* know. And it surprises you. And when you say you didn't know, that surprise is evident in your voice.

"Well, it's not a big deal he didn't tell you, right?"

Skrrrrrt. Let's pause. Because what R just did is *very* uncool. And something you should never do. Is it possible Weckea *told* her to tell you? Yes. But let's presume he didn't. In which case, R has done a Very Bad Thing that has the potential to negatively impact your relationship with Weckea. For one, it could very well put you in your feelings that he *didn't* tell you. And is that really fair? It's his business to share or not share things about himself based on whether or not he feels safe doing so.

Because that's the other thing: It could also negatively impact your relationship by shifting the way you *see* Weckea based on biases you may not even realize you have. And that's almost what happens.

(**Narrator Nic shakes fist at R.**)

Because though we've acknowledged that the you who arrives at Temple is both racist and sexist, we now need to acknowledge that you are—again, by default—also homophobic.

Similar to that of the majority of people born in the twentieth century, your homophobia is a function of what basically amounts to erasure; your parents rarely even acknowledged the *existence* of non-heterosexual people, let alone talked about members of the LGBTQIAP+ community in depth. Once you add *exceedingly* trash rhetoric about homosexuality pulled from English translations of the Bible—rhetoric seeded into the foundations of our great nation and frequently used to substantiate dangerous and untrue stereotypes about Rainbow People (as *I* like to call us)—

it's fair to say you are a homophobic hot mess waiting to happen. *Most* of us are.

In fact, when you first start interacting with Kaila, Yaba, Weckea, and Monica (whom we'll get to shortly), you are actually *more* than homophobic. Because, as implied above, the orientation spectrum isn't limited to heterosexual or homosexual / straight or gay. And because *most* people, you included, are raised to believe that heterosexual is the only "right" way to be, *any* other orientation, like lesbian, bisexual, and pansexual, is "wrong" by default. Which means it wouldn't hurt to use a term that's more . . . *expansive* than "homophobic."

Thankfully (because, let's be honest, "not-hetero-phobic" ain't the move), there is one: queerphobic.

The word *queer* has its own fascinating history—it's a **reclaimed slur**, in fact—but we won't get too deep into that right now. What you need to know about it at *this* juncture in your journey is that by the time you reach the 2020s, *queer* will be the accepted blanket term for "non-heterosexual" and/or "non-cisgender." An adjective to describe Rainbow People.

And just like with gender, a new and grotesque monster rears its double head at the race-orientation intersection: **queer racist ideas**.

Queer racist idea: Any notion that suggests that one race-orientation is superior or inferior to another race-orientation in any way, or justifies policies that lead to injustice or inequity between race-orientations.

Example:
Lesbian, gay, bisexual, trans, queer, intersex, asexual, pansexual, plus—because there are myriad other ways non-hetero and/or non-cisgender people choose to identify (nonbinary, genderqueer, heteroflexible, biromantic, etc.). Though there's no single word that encompasses all of these identities, there is a symbol: the rainbow, frequently with black and brown, and/or pastel-pink, white, and pastel-blue stripes added.

Queerphobic stereotypes abound, but most of the ones that rise to the top of your mind upon learning of Weckea's orientation are specific to Black gay men. Like:

- Black gay men run around having unprotected sex all the time. (*Weckea doesn't seem sex crazed or reckless* is something that pops into your head to counter this one.)
- The hypersexuality and recklessness of Black gay men are the reasons so many Black gay men contract HIV. (*And don't* most *Black gay men contract HIV?* you think.)
- All Black gay men are visibly "effeminate" and easy to identify as gay on sight—though that "femininity" is inauthentic.

All of these myths get debunked as you realize that choosing between your queerphobia (specifically *homophobia* in this case) and your friendship with Weckea is a no-brainer, and you get to work unlearning the foolishness you didn't even realize you'd learned in the first place. Some of these myth busters include:

- Black gay men are *less* likely to have unprotected sex than White gay men. And are also less likely to use illicit drugs, which heighten the risk of HIV infections, during sexual encounters.
- The race-orientation-gender inequities in HIV-positivity rates have far more to do with **racist policies** than with "deviant" behavior in queer communities of color. (And *most* Black gay men do *not* contract HIV.)

- Not all Black gay men (or all of *any* racialized gay male group, for that matter) "act like women," and . . .
- The ones who *do* move and speak in ways that are typically equated with femininity are not "pretending" or doing so *in*authentically.

This last one clicks for you as a result of hanging out with that other friend I mentioned: Monica, a more "masculine"-presenting Black lesbian from Texas. You and Monica talk about women the way you *expected* to be able to talk to Weckea (and the irony isn't lost on you). In fact, talking to Monica about your romantic experiences feels similar to talking with the straight-dude friends you had at FAMU. And the more you get to know Monica, the more you realize that her masculinity—or at least what *you* would label as masculinity—isn't an act. She just is who she is.

The same goes for Weckea, who you never would've guessed is gay.

And same goes for the guys in your FAMU modeling troupe, who you presumed to be gay based on the way they moved, spoke, and looked.

Like gender racist ideas, queer racist ideas also have to be uprooted in order for one to be truly antiracist. Opposing racism but failing/refusing to address queerphobia completely undermines all attempts at being antiracist because ignoring policies that negatively impact queer people means allowing inequities between race-orientations—and therefore inequities between racial groups—to endure. There is no separating race from orientation or choosing to accept one but not the other, because there is no separating the identity markers of individual human beings into definable parts and deciding which parts you'll keep and which parts you'll throw away. *Whole* people must be accepted wholly.

To be antiracist, *all* Black lives have to matter to you, including the queer ones. *All* Asian hate must be stopped, not just that aimed at straight, cisgender Asian people. We must fight for the rights of gay Latino men as resoundingly as we fight for straight Latina women.

And thankfully for you, Kaila and Yaba will make this *so* clear, you'll never forget it.

A WORD ABOUT PATRIARCHAL WOMEN AND QUEERPHOBIC QUEER PEOPLE

Yep. You read that right.

This is the thing about status quos and systems of oppression: They pop out as little gremlin-esque babies. Because sexist and queerphobic ideas (along with racist and ableist ones) function as interlocking cogs that keep the status quo turning as smoothly as the earth on its axis, *everyone* is susceptible to them. Including the people those ideas negatively impact.

We've touched on this regarding racism—remember Mr. Editor at that Tallahassee newspaper who was a Black anti-Black racist? Well, because sexist patriarchy and queerphobia are also deeply embedded in the US status quo, women and queer people can subscribe to sexist and/or queerphobic ideas, often without even realizing it. ALL marginalized people can—and sometimes do.

> **Internalized oppression:** When members of a marginalized group accept and/or reaffirm negative stereotypes against their own group and come to believe and/or act as though the belief system, values, and way of life of the dominant group are correct.

There are women who believe—subconsciously or overtly—that other women are "catty" or "overly emotional," neither of which has *any* grounding in data or reality. This contributes to the (false) notion that men are "more levelheaded" and therefore "more qualified" for leadership roles. Thus, gender inequities in high-level leadership roles persist and women contribute to the sexist discrimination that results in things like the gender wage gap.

Various forms of internalized queerphobia—e.g., homophobia, biphobia, and transphobia—have a similar impact and result in nasties like queerphobic discrimination in the workplace and the perpetuation of myths that consistently land children's stories that feature queer characters on banned-books lists . . . and therefore out of the hands of the queer kids who need to see themselves represented and their existence normalized.

Internalized oppression also contributes to—and can be the result of—one of *the* most devious status quo perpetuators:

> **Tokenism:** A forced form of diversity that involves including, recruiting, or hiring a small number of people from underrepresented groups to create the superficial appearance of equity or equality.

So, yes, choosing to be antiracist is good for the world, and it honors the other human beings who inhabit it. But if you're marginalized in any way—and *you* certainly are—committing to the antiracist act of recognizing and uprooting all forms of internalized oppression is also good for *you*.

- 13 -

CLASS

All righty. Back to Temple.

Actually, rewind. You graduate from Stonewall Jackson High School in Manassas, Virginia, then complete your undergraduate studies at Florida A&M University (go, Rattlers!) in Tallahassee, Florida. Temple means a move to a new city: Philadelphia. And you couldn't be more thrilled.

You pick a neighborhood in the northern part of town, called Hunting Park. And though you love it, people look at you sideways when they hear where you *decided* to plant yourself, and even your parents are none too thrilled.

They hear what the people living in Hunting Park have been told for years: This is one of the most dangerous neighborhoods in Philadelphia. Low-income. High rates of interpersonal violence.

The "ghetto."

Then (2005), as now, when people hear that word, it conjures a very specific set of images and ideas. Often at the center of these ideas/images? Black people. Living in either tall tenement buildings of government-subsidized apartments—the "Projects"—or areas full of run-down houses, some of which are presumed to be nexuses of drug trafficking and/or gang activity.

Long forgotten are the origins of *ghetto*. Which, in and of themselves, are rather troubling: Christians in early-sixteenth-century Venice wanted the city to be Christian-*only,* so in a bizarre "compromise," the city shoved its entire Jewish population into a small island in the northern part of the city known as the "New Ghetto." It's assumed that the word came from *gettare,* which meant "to pour" or "to cast" and likely had to do with the fact that there had been a copper foundry in that area before the Jewish people were more or less exiled there.

Time rolled. More physically enclosed—and legally mandatory—exclusively Jewish areas started popping up in cities all around Italy. The name for the Venetian one apparently traveled well: All of the new ones were also called *ghettos.* And though these wretched little bubbles of banishment were eventually dismantled—the last one standing was the ghetto of Rome, and it was dissolved in 1870—the name stuck.

It was used for big-city neighborhoods full of Jewish immigrants here in the United States (like the "New York Ghetto" of the Lower East Side) and was eventually overtaken by the Nazis to delineate sites of forced Jewish segregation during World War II. Sites that were plagued by starvation and rife with disease and that eventually saw mass deportations to death camps and killing fields.

It was in the mid-1960s—in the thick of the Civil Rights Movement—when "urban" segregated areas in cities across the country were shoved into headlines, and "Negro ghetto" and "Black ghetto" began to eclipse "Jewish ghetto." And partially as the result of a book called *Dark Ghetto* by African American psychologist Kenneth Clark.

The point here: The notion of "the ghetto" as a fairly homogenous place (read: segregated, whether legally or not) ain't new. The word has always had a "less-than" connotation. It has *always* suggested that the people who live *in* the ghetto are inferior to the ones who don't.

What *you're* coming to discover as you settle into living *in* "the ghetto" is that the stuff everyone seems to fear and mock is inextricably linked to poverty . . . and rooted in racism. Thus, a pair of new (for you, at least) intersectional concepts emerges: that of the **race-class** and that of **class racism**.

Race-class: A grouping of people at the intersection of race and class.	**Example:** *Native poor, Black elites, White middle class*

Class racist idea: Any notion that suggests a **race-class** is superior or inferior to another **race-class** in any way, to justify the relative disparities in poverty and wealth between the **race-classes** brought on by **racial capitalism**.

Let's break that down:

You have classes—elite, middle, poor. And you have races. "Poor people are lazy" is a classist statement. "Black people are lazy" is a racist statement. "Poor Black people are the laziest" is an expression of a **class racist idea**.

So. This notion people have of "ghetto" as poor, Black, irresponsible, indecent, and uncivilized, and "the ghetto" as a place populated by "ghetto" people? **Class racist ideas** at their finest.

And just like with all other iterations of racism, *anyone* can subscribe to **class racist** ideas. What's interesting here is that those ideas can go in multiple directions. Over the course of your graduate studies, you'll witness Black elites and elites of color looking down their noses at the poor in their own racial group as well as in other racial groups, White included; we've read about "them n*****s," but "White trash" is also a thing.

And *also* like with all other iterations of racism, racist ideas root the problem—and the resulting racial inequities—in the people.

NIC'S NOTES:
Based on the definition of racist ideas we're working with here, any person—White people included—who lumps all poor White people together—ascribing the behavior of a poor White individual to *all* poor White people, or viewing an individual poor White person through the lens of ideas about the group—is expressing class racist ideas.

Since 1959, when an anthropologist named Oscar Lewis completed an ethnographic study of Mexican families and blessed (not) the world with the (backward) concept of a "culture of poverty," racist elitists turned their eyes to the behavior of poor people, especially poor Black people and poor people of color, to explain why they can't seem to get un-poor. Observe these two quotes:

"People with a culture of poverty . . . are a marginal people who know only their own troubles, their own local conditions, their own neighborhood, their own way of life." —Oscar Lewis, 1963

"We have got this tailspin of culture in our inner cities in particular of men not working, and just generations of men not even thinking about working, and not learning the value and the culture of work." —Congressman (and eventual Speaker of the House) Paul Ryan, 2014

And as per usual with this stuff, what gets brushed under the rug are the **racist policies** that created the inequitable conditions in the first place. What began as redlining in the 1930s hasn't ever stopped.

Crash course: Redlining was a system of government and banking policies that refused to provide and insure mortgages in and near African American neighborhoods. But funds were shoveled into the hands of builders producing subdivisions for White people . . . under the stipulation that none of those homes be sold to Black people, which would allegedly tank property values.

And now, *because* of racist policies, a *cycle* of poverty persists and makes getting *out* of poverty incredibly difficult. Low incomes and limited opportunities for earning more compound with unfair economic practices, like higher cost of living in more "desirable" areas that jack up the prices of homes. And this is on *top* of things like tax cuts for corporations (read:

NIC'S NOTES:
For the record, the opposite was true; because Black people were willing to pay MORE for homes in these lily-White neighborhoods—a result of Black housing options being so limited—the property values *rose*.

already-rich people) and big-business bailouts that benefit the elite (again: already-rich people).

The wildest thing, though: You'll *also* see class racism flow in the opposite direction, with poor and/or middle-class Black people and people of color subscribing to class racist ideas about Black elites and elites of color.

In fact, for a time, *you* lean into some of these class racist ideas. It's part of the reason you decide to live in Hunting Park. Based on ideas that emerged in the late 1950s, *authentic* Blackness involves hardship. Struggle. Overt opposition to assimilation and respectability. Experiences that can only be found outside of the White gaze, in the ghetto. According to *this* **class racist idea**, Black elites are sellouts who pander to White people while exploiting their *own* people for both financial gain and White approval. You choose Hunting Park because you've bought into the idea that elite *and* middle-class Black people, yourself included, are spoiled and need to be reminded of what it *really* means to be Black in the United States.

To be antiracist is to dispense with the notion that *any* race-class is superior to any other, whether within a single racial group or across racial groupings. To be antiracist is to see all people of all classes as inherently equal.

- 14 -

CULTURE

Okay, now we gotta rewind again. Because though we know that fateful MLK speech competition takes place when you're a high school senior in Manassas, Virginia, the last time we saw you pre-grad school, you were in Queens, New York, grappling with life in a body you're both fearful *for* and fearful *of.*

So how do you go from standing on a city bus with a guy called Smurf grinning as he points a gun at you to standing in a pulpit, remixing Dr. King's dream? Let's take it back to John Bowne High School in 1996.

You're not sure how—maybe it's the difficulty you have separating the harassing police officer from the harassing teacher, or maybe it's your increased awareness of the disdain from educators who fear your growing Black body and feel it more fitting for prison than their learning institution—but at some point during the first few months of freshman year, your indifference toward school morphs into outright hatred. It could be your puberty-based shifting awareness of your body—and the world's seeming fear of it, as evidenced by the way cops harass you *and* the way teachers seem to have preemptively decided you're up to no good. It could be your new environment and the taxing nature of your constant vigilance when it comes to the bodies around you.

What you know for sure is that you're not allowed to fail any classes if you want to stay on the junior varsity basketball team. You have to post two Cs and three Ds to even be able to pick up the ball. So . . . that's what you do.

Two Cs.

Three Ds.

What you *love*, though (other than basketball, that is): the Ave. Named for the intersection at Jamaica Avenue and 164th Street, the area referred to as "the Ave" encompasses a couple dozen city blocks and is a shopping district constantly packed with teens just like you who come to see and be seen.

There are outfits and sneakers to admire and/or critique. Music blasting from multiple directions. Budding poets who choose hip-hop as their medium of delivery. It's a cultural wonderland. And one that makes sense to you. The Ave is a place where you feel like you *belong*. Your personal mecca. And you hop in a cab to make your way down the thirty-six blocks between your house and the Ave as often as Ma and Dad will allow it.

Why?

> **Culture:** The sum total way of life, including shared beliefs, customs, and art forms, created and recreated by a group of people and transmitted from one generation to another.

The Ave feels more welcoming than school—feels like *home*, even—because everything about what you encounter there makes sense to you. The food, the clothes, the music, the language, the mannerisms. It's the epitome, for you, of African American culture. *Your* culture.

Sadly, though, not everyone appreciates African American

culture the way you do. In fact, *many* people—some of them Black—see the culture you love so much as inferior to and derivative of the "dominant" culture. Observe:

- Language. The way you and your friends on the Ave speak—mostly to one another, mind you—is deemed "broken," "improper," or "nonstandard" English. In fact, in *most* places, languages created by enslaved Africans in European colonies were (and *are*) treated this way. African American Ebonics (or African American Vernacular English [AAVE], depending on who you ask), Jamaican Patois, Haitian Creole, Brazilian Calunga, Cubano . . . all of these African languages—you know, because they were created by African people and have been sustained by said people's descendants—have been deemed "incorrect" by **racist power**.
- Style. On the Ave—and on your own body—T-shirts and sports jerseys are oversized, and jeans are worn baggy with a slight sag. Gold chains covered in sparkling gemstones, be they actual diamonds or cubic zirconias, dangle from necks; ears are pierced across the gender spectrum, and skin is inked . . . And every single last bit of it gets associated with "thuggery," or jail culture. That's not to mention the many female-presenting people your age who choose to wear clothes that are short or tight or otherwise revealing of the body parts they want to flaunt. Which gets them called "fast" and sexualized like adult women.
- Music. Bass-heavy, expressive of everything from frustration with the police to desire for physical inti-

macy to celebration of self and/or upward mobility, and usually cranked up loud, the literal* poetry that is hip-hop and R&B comprises the soundtrack for your movement through the world. A soundtrack that's heavily denounced by **racist power**.

*Yes, literal. Think about it: The widely accepted definition of poetry is something along the lines of a rhythmical composition, written or spoken, designed to engender emotion through the expression of feelings and/or ideas. Which would mean the vast majority of music with lyrics–hip-hop and R&B included–is literal poetry.

You encounter African American culture on the Ave and in the expressions of faith—body swaying, hands waving, sinners and saints alike shouting and leaping to their feet—at your church. You embrace it in the way you style your hair and the foods you choose to eat. The language you use. The way you greet people who look like you. Your manner of interacting with your elders.

And there's a good chance that your discomfort at—and hatred of—school is rooted in the very clear message you receive there: Your culture is not only wrong, but it's also worthy of little more than constant criticism and disdain.

As you know by now, ideas of what constitute "civilization" are the bedrock of racist ideas, both historical and modern. These notions of what is and isn't "civilized" are used to create a cultural hierarchy, with (loosely) European-based cultures at the top, waiting to be aspired to—Assimilation 101—and everybody else's culture . . . beneath that.

And *that* is a cultural racist idea.

Cultural racist idea: Any notion that creates a cultural standard and imposes a cultural hierarchy among racial groups.

Let's debunk some of the racist myths about African American culture above. Debunking that can be applied to *all* iterations of cultural racist ideas.

- Language. There is no "correct" English. Language is a human creation designed for ease of communication and transmission of meaning, and it is *constantly* changing. In other words: *We* are the masters of language, not the other way around. *We* determine how language is used and what form it takes in our everyday lives, and it is *entirely normal* for those uses and forms to vary based on where we are, who we're talking to, what we're talking about, and in what format (Spoken? Written? Communicated with our hands like in sign *language*?). The best part: If the person you're communicating with understands what you're expressing, you have communicated effectively. Full stop.

- Style. There is no "inferior" or "incorrect" or "universally proper" or "moral" way to dress.

  Example:
  The hijab, a headscarf worn by many Muslim women, or the dastār, a turban worn by Sikh men

  Like language, fashion is a human creation used for self-expression and *intra*-cultural conveyance of meaning.

- Music. Same as the two above: human creation. No "right" or "wrong." There is personal preference, of course—you prefer hip-hop to death metal, for instance—but all music is enjoyable to *someone*. And that's all that matters.

There's no "incorrect" expression of faith or "standard" way to interact with other members of your cultural group. No culture is better or more civilized than any other culture. And there is, therefore, no need to assimilate to meet some imaginary "proper" cultural ideal.

Which you *know* when it comes to the way White people look at you as you move through the hallways of John Bowne High in Queens, New York . . .

But once you move south to Manassas, Virginia?

It's safe to say your *own* **cultural racist ideas** bubble right on up to the surface.

Manassas is tough for you at first. Your parents, under the influence of your Aunt Rena, move your family to a house in a White suburban neighborhood. And spoiler alert: With your baggy clothes, (clean) Air Force 1s and/or Timbs, swaggerish strut, and very *not-*southern accent, you don't *fit in*.

Stonewall Jackson High School is *very* not John Bowne. But despite feeling like two different planets, they have one thing in common: a basketball team.

One you initially don't make.

(**Insert broken heart and crying face emojis.** Anachronistic, but appropriate here.)

You literally cry to Dad about it.

But as you'll later come to recognize, there's more going on here than you not being good enough to make the team. You *are* good enough. Let's not forget, you're warming up for a Stonewall Jackson *varsity* game when Dad busts onto the court, waving your Hampton University acceptance letter in the air.

So what gives?

Well, from the moment you cross the Virginia state line, you've got your nose in the air when it comes to your estimation of non-urban southern African American culture.

You can't stand the way these country Black southerners talk. Or dress. Their slang is corny, and their music is wack. And these **cultural racist ideas** of *yours* flowed right onto the basketball court. Because, based in part on your disdain for the iterations of African American culture surrounding you in Virginia (or racialized southern culture, depending on how you look at it), you assumed the other guys trying out were trash, and you played down to them. The arrogance flowed off you like post-practice funk.

You gone learn, though.

For now, we'll leave you with a quote to be inspired by and a definition to aspire to:

"All cultures must be judged in relation to their own history, and all individuals and groups in relation to their cultural history, and definitely not by the arbitrary standard of any single culture." —Ashley Montagu

> **Cultural antiracist idea:** Any notion that rejects cultural standards and equalizes cultural differences among racial groups.

A WORD ABOUT CULTURAL APPROPRIATION

Yeah, it's definitely a mouthful.

And when the concept comes to the fore of social consciousness in the mid-2010s—driven pretty heavily by White pop stars/celebrities wearing hairstyles with very specific historical implications—you're going to hear a lot of people say it's not *really* a thing.

So what if a White pop star decides to rock giant gold bamboo earrings, a gold chain necklace, and booty shorts in one video scene—elements of late-1980s and early-1990s Fly Girl culture, popularized in large part by lady hip-hop duo Salt-N-Pepa—and in another scene (same video) is strutting around with a boom box on her shoulder in an outfit heavily reminiscent of B-boy culture, birthed by Black and Latinx anti–status quo dancers in 1970s New York?

It's just clothes, right?

So what if a different White pop star pops up in *her* video with her straight brown hair in cornrows and her *edges laid*—the hair at her hairline and temples slicked down into a wavelike design? It's just hair. And so what if this same pop star dressed up like a geisha in a different video? It's no big deal.

So what if some White music lovers don sacred Native American–style headdresses at music festivals and wear them in lingerie runway shows? And if other White entertainers wear bindis and incorporate bhangra into their live performances?

What. Is. The. Big. Deal?

Well, it has a lot to do with power, respect, and attribution.

Cultural appropriation: The act of performing or com-modifying cultural identity markers, including language, traditions, and style, from communities of color in a way that is stereotypical, disrespectful, and/or inauthentic.

Is borrowing elements of other people's cultures always wrong? Of course not. Do things get a bit hairy when borrowed cultural elements are turned into sources of profit for White people? Absolutely.

But what tends to bother people of color the most about this "borrowing" is that it's a one-way street; only members of the dominant culture can cherry-pick which elements they want to "borrow" from marginalized cultures and which cultural elements will be a source of continued marginalization. The same person who decides to wear cornrows like yours might feel threatened and pull out a gun if they see you wearing a hoodie.

At the end of the day, the most important thing to reflect upon is this: Being antiracist *does* involve respectfully enjoying and appreci-ating the cultures of other racialized groups . . . but that appreciation must involve the *totality* of cultures to truly be antiracist. Deciding to appreciate some aspects of another group's culture while rejecting or denouncing other aspects misses the mark.

Because really: Can one truly call themselves antiracist yet be okay with the "appreciating" and "enjoying" the elements of other people's cultures deemed likeable while simultaneously rejecting the people with whom those "likeable" elements originate?

Being able to perform someone else's culture is one thing. Being able to empathize with the people who created the culture? That's another thing entirely.

- 15 -

SPACE

And no, we're not talking about *outer* space (though it *would* be cool if places like the Intergalactic Empire of Wakanda actually existed). As a student at Temple University, you'll come to enjoy, appreciate, and understand the importance of a different type of space. One that's labeled as a result of being considered *other* than the norm.

The Black space.

You grow up in Black spaces. They are spaces either governed by Black people, Black thoughts, Black cultures, Black histories, and Black traditions, OR spaces inhabited mostly by Black people. For the bulk of kindergarten through undergrad at Florida A&M University, you learn in Black spaces.

But it's during your time at Temple—an integrated White space where you find yourself in the microcosmic Black space of your African American Studies program—that you absorb the ethos and movement and comprehension of racialized spaces to the point where you're able to define, dissect, and discuss them.

You feel most at home in the Black spaces that are majority Black *and* governed by Black people, ideas, traditions, etc. And most *not* at home in majority-White spaces that run on Eurocentric versions of the same stuff.

But there's a thorny third area that highlights how **space racism** functions. Remember that gripe you had with that teacher whose name you can't remember because she clearly favored the three

White students in your predominantly Black third-grade class? Or the school you walked through with your parents where the class pictures featured all Black faces except for the teacher? Or how at John Bowne, which was full to the brim with kids who had varying shades of your skin tone, you always felt stalked by something intangible but insidious?

It's because *those* spaces, while filled with Black (and sometimes Brown) bodies, weren't governed by Black people, Black thoughts, Black cultures, Black histories, or Black traditions. In fact, the guiding principles in *every* educational space you attended prior to undergrad were governed by Whiteness: White thoughts, White ideas of what constitutes right and wrong, White histories, White traditions, White teachers and administrators. So in these very Black-*looking* spaces, you and everyone around you were expected to live up to White-space standards.

Except then, as now, people would be reluctant to call the source of these standards "White spaces." Because for as long as **racism** has been a thing, *White* spaces have been considered not only superior, but universal—the standard for how *all* spaces should operate.

This is the crux of **space racist ideas**.

> **Space racist idea:** Any notion that suggests that a racialized space is superior or inferior to another racialized space in any way, or justifies policies that lead to injustice or resource inequity between racialized spaces or the elimination of certain racialized spaces.

The African American Studies doctoral program you're a part of at Temple was founded in 1987 by Molefi Kete Asante. He created it as a space where Black students such as yourself could move and learn outside the conditioned confines of Eurocentric standardization. Asante—and his right-hand woman, Professor Ama Mazama—are the epitome of anti-assimilationist. "The rejection of European particularism as universal is the first stage of our coming intellectual struggle," Asante wrote.

NIC'S NOTES:
In other words, the *European way* shouldn't be the standard for doing things right.

And it genuinely is a Whole Thing, European particularism. One that has convinced people across the *globe* that White is synonymous with colorless.

But it isn't. Even in a scientific sense, white isn't the "absence of color" any more than black would be. White *is* a color. And in a racist world, *everyone's* experiences are impacted by their race, White people included. It's through this realization that you come to embrace one of Asante's central ideas (as taught to you by Mazama): Objectivity, the notion of being fact based and uninfluenced by personal feelings, interpretations, or prejudice, is just collective (grand-scale) *sub*jectivity, which is enough people agreeing on a thing to make it "normal" and therefore seemingly universal and able to be standardized.

Collective subjectivity is the source of **racist power**. Enough people of European descent agreed that their way of life was *the* Way of Life and deemed any *other* way of life not only inferior, but subhuman. To drive this idea home, some of them enslaved individuals from cultural and ethnic backgrounds that didn't meet the standard and then spread the word of those groups' inferiority . . . which, by default, further strengthened the idea of European superiority, and European culture/traditions/thoughts/ideas as the ideal everyone should aspire to.

Which means that when spaces *aren't* governed by this so-called universal standard, especially here in these United States, those spaces are seen as suspect (or even deviant, depending on who you're talking to). Sometimes even to the people who inhabit them. Entire Black neighborhoods are stigmatized as places of violence, danger, and death because they're filled with Black people, but most mass shooters come out of White neighborhoods, which are viewed as "safe" simply because they're filled with White people. White spaces get elevated, and *non*-White spaces get denigrated.

You observe this from multiple directions:

- Seeing how hard the security personnel of Temple University work to keep the campus—a White space made up of a collection of buildings—"safe" within its "dangerous" Northern Philadelphia neighborhood, a low-income Black space.
- Feeling the ire of White students and faculty at Temple who wear their disdain of the Black space that is your African American Studies department like a grody old coat.
- Hearing not only people on campus, but even Ma and Dad express their "concern" over your decision to live in the Black space that is Hunting Park.
- Nashay, the only person in your all-Black African American Studies department who expressed nothing but hatred for the HBCU* Black space she graduated from.

*HBCU stands for Historically Black Colleges and Universities.

Nashay's perspective on her HBCU Black space is a point of contention for you. And not at all because you're an ever-benevolent king in the glorious land of antiracism and you see all racialized spaces as equal and legitimate at this point. It's because Nashay went to the same school that you did for undergrad: Florida A&M University.

She complains about the alleged incompetence of FAMU's faculty and administration. This is based on the error of a single individual in a single office on the entire campus, which suggests that her conclusion that the university harbored incompetence was already there in her mind somewhere, and the single error served as biased confirmation of a thing she already believed.

But it's Nashay's lowly opinion of FAMU that highlights the **space racist ideas** hiding in *your* own thinking. You've not only heard what she was saying before, you've said it yourself. You too complained about the HBCU administration and had the thought that the people running the show were incompetent. You heard Black students and faculty members at historically White colleges and universities—HWCUs*—refer to HBCUs as "ghetto" and say they could never go to one. You heard students at your own HBCU—not unlike Nashay—complain about how badly run the university was and threaten to leave for White schools.

And you continue to hear people, Black and White alike, argue that HBCUs—and Black spaces as a whole—don't represent "the real world" and therefore fail to prepare students for "real life." The idea,

*W for *White*, obviously. Historically White colleges and universities in the United States were founded specifically for White students. For reference, seven of the eight Ivy League universities were founded between 1636 and 1769, and Dartmouth was the first to admit a Black student, in 1824. The first African American on record to attend an American college or university was John Chavis in 1799. He didn't graduate.

which is relatively simple and low-key, seems pretty logical: Black students and students of color are better served by majority-White institutions of higher education because they'll better prepare them to function in a majority-White world.

The underlying issue here, though? This seemingly *logical* idea conflates the "real world" with a White, Eurocentric worldview. In other words, it poses that the only *legitimate* world is one governed by White ideas, White thoughts, White histories, White traditions, and White people. A world where assimilation is the only viable option because White standards are considered ultimate and supreme.

This **space racist idea**—again: White spaces as superior to all other spaces—justifies flagrant racial inequities throughout the course of American history. The *Brown vs. Board of Education* Supreme Court decision outlawed segregation in public schools, which forced (superior) White educational spaces to open their doors to Black children, who were then *freed* from the "dark ghettos" that were Black educational spaces where kids were said to have underperformed or dropped out from before reaching middle school.

To this day, permissive transfers and desegregation busing programs cart Black and Latinx students away from the "bad schools" in their "ghetto" neighborhoods and deposit them in "high-performing" White school districts. Incredible Black teachers take their talents to White schools, where the pay is better and the students are "better behaved."

When the ruling was handed down that segregated schools were unconstitutional, Chief Justice Earl Warren wrote that the "segregation of white and colored children in public schools has a detrimental effect upon the colored children" and that it "has a tendency to [delay] the educational and mental development of negro children."

The fact that the collective solution to this problem was to allow Black children into White spaces sends a pretty powerful message:

White spaces are the only places Black children can *really* grow and develop in.

What will occur to you as you make your way through grad school: Black spaces themselves aren't inherently inferior. Black teachers aren't less qualified to mold minds than White teachers, and Black students aren't inherently less intelligent than White students. Majority-Black and/or -Latinx public school buildings aren't in need of repairs because they're full of "unruly" Black and/or Latinx children. The real reason for inequality between White schools and schools of color, like many other racial inequities, comes down to the unequal distribution of resources—a direct result of **space racist ideas**.

So what's the antiracist move here? Well, it starts with the recognition that differences in racialized spaces have less to do with the races of the people in the spaces and more to do with persistent racial inequity—resulting from **racist policies**—in every area, from educational resources to job access to incarceration rates.

Then it's vital to recognize *all* racialized spaces as both legitimate and inherently equal in their differences. Because the real world isn't White. It's as varied as the cultures, traditions, ethnicities, and skin tones that make it a place worth living in.

Part Three

UPSIDE DOWN: FLIPPING THE WORLD OVER

All forms of racism are overt if our antiracist eyes are open
to seeing racist policy in racial inequity.

—Dr. Ibram X. Kendi, *How to Be an Antiracist*

16

FAILURE → SUCCESS

So.

You've gone through the inside stuff, picking apart how you've been conditioned to think about the world and the people in it, yourself included. You've also turned outward and begun to examine all the ways racism manifests itself, often entangling with other forms of oppression. You're now aware of the dueling consciousness and how it confuses things, as well as the differences between antiracist ideas, as well as segregationist and assimilationist ideas—both of which are racist because they look to Whiteness as the "correct" and supreme standard.

You've started the process of getting your mind right, and you're bouncing on your toes, ready to get in the ring and hit racism with a one-two punch.

What now?

Well, as you'll come to discover in 2007, actually *getting things done* ain't easy. In fact, you're about to fail pretty miserably.

Background: In September 2006, a Black student at a high school in Jena, Louisiana, asked if he could sit under a tree. The "white tree" as it came to be known in the media. The next day, students arrived at school to find that three nooses had been hung in said tree. Whether this was a prank or a warning didn't actually matter; it was racist.

The perpetrators were suspended.

Fast-forward to December of the same year. Six Black students—including a star football player—beat up a White kid. All six were arrested and charged with attempted murder and conspiracy to commit murder.

A charge that carried a penalty of up to one hundred years in prison. Which is what the district attorney said he would seek.

In September 2007, you're sitting at a professor's desk at Temple University, revving up to start your Black Student Union (BSU) meeting, during which you intend to share the plans for a campaign that you hope will help free the six Black boys—dubbed the Jena Six—in Louisiana.

By this point, an all-White jury has already found Mychal Bell, the star football player, guilty of aggravated battery. A conviction that could carry up to a twenty-two-year sentence in prison.

But even that is too much. All over the country, Black people are in an uproar over what seem to be excessive charges slapped down on these six boys by a racist judicial system in what is clearly a racist place (remember the nooses?). You are also enraged. So you start the meeting by explaining the 106 Campaign to Free the Jena Six: (1) Mobilize at least 106 students on each of 106 campuses—a minimum of 11,236 students total—to rally locally for the sake of raising money for the Jena Six legal-defense fund, and (2) Marshal those thousands of students into car caravans that would converge in Washington, DC, on October 5, 2007. The cars would park, and the students would march together to the Department of Justice, where you would present your six demands of freedom.

It's a no-go—the BSU officers vote the whole thing down and opt for a smaller, local march instead. And to you, this is a sign that your BSU peers are ignorant about racism and how it functions. Which is something you refuse to be. Your cohorts might be failures, but you certainly aren't.

Except . . . you are. As are many who choose to be antiracist but then put their gloves on and step into the wrong ring. Because even with allllll the self-interrogating and uprooting and relearning you've done up to this point, you, like many who came before you and many who will come after, have been training based on faulty information about the opponent.

For instance, while **race**, like marriage and religion and family, *is* a social construct in that it's a thing because people agree that it is, it's also a ***power*** construct. The people who *created* it did so to give themselves power, and the people who uphold it do so to *keep* power—which means you can't just change it or get rid of it by changing the minds of the people on the ground.

Another thing: History isn't, and has never been, a straight-line march of forward progress; it's always been more of a zigzaggy back-and-forth battle between antiracist progress (e.g., the implementation of Affirmative Action policies) and racist progress (e.g., the imposition of highly restrictive voter registration laws that disproportionately limit voters of color, particularly Black voters.)

And then one that's maaaad difficult to get our heads around: The **race** problem isn't rooted in ignorance and hate. It's *rooted*—like how a tree is rooted—in powerful self-interest: People who benefit from it keep it going to keep benefitting.

NIC'S NOTES:
Though ignorance and hate DO keep the ball rolling, now! Let's not get it twisted!

The problem with your initial approach regarding the Jena Six is that it is focused on pointing at and shouting about the massive tree of racism—"Look!" you're practically screaming. "LOOK at this monstrosity! It needs to be brought down!"—for the sake of getting others to join you in punching and kicking at its gigantic, unbending trunk.

Years later, you're going to meet a queen named Sadiqa. And there will come a night when you and Sadiqa are on a date at a restaurant that has a massive golden statue of the Buddha inside it. And you're going to watch a drunk White dude approach that statue and defile it with an inappropriate gesture, more or less putting on a Very Hilarious Show for his Very Drunk White Dude friends.

You will ignore it. But Sadiqa will be unable to. And the conversation that ensues between you and this queen will highlight what being in the wrong boxing ring looks like:

"At least he's not Black," Sadiqa says.

"How would you feel if he were Black?" you ask her (and also yourself).

"I'd be really embarrassed," she says . . . also answering for you. "Because we don't need anyone making us look bad."

"In front of White people?" (Though you already know the answer.)

"Yes," comes Sadiqa's reply. "It makes them look down on us. ***Makes them more racist.****"*

And therein lies the most insidious falsehood about the Great Opponent: That people like you who are on the short end of the inequity stick *and* trying to beat back the beast creating the injustice (**racism**, in case that wasn't clear) must do so while also being on your best behavior.

Share your experiences and say what you think and how you feel . . . but only using rhetoric that won't offend or "alienate" White people. Make your signs and gather your friends and go march or whatnot, but don't be *too* disruptive . . . like, don't overtake any freeways or do anything illegal. Make your social media posts, but don't say anything that might have people looking at you funny in school.

With this tactic (which is another manifestation of the dueling consciousness), you will *FAIL every single time.*

The worst thing about this? Eventually, those failures add up, and many who have chosen to be antiracist, you included, will begin to lean into another false idea about what we're up against.

If you noticed, I, your ever-epic narrator, have used two different metaphors for racism in this chapter: that of a solidly rooted, thickly trunked tree, and that of a boxing opponent. No, I'm not confused and mixing my literary devices . . . Each metaphor represents a distinct ideology about racism. One is resoundingly false and dooms budding antiracists like yourself to failure. But the other one? It's not only true, it's *actionable*.

Observe:

It's 2010. You've finished that doctorate at Temple and have officially been *Dr.* Ibram X. Kendi for, like . . . a few days. Which is *huge*. You've metamorphosed from a reluctant classroom occupant to a bona fide *professor* and career academic. HUGE! And you're sitting in a lecture at SUNY Oneonta that centers on the idea of racism as a disease.

And you're not with it.

Your hand flies up. "Instead of describing racism as a disease, don't you think racism is more like an organ?" you ask the lecturer. "Isn't racism essential for America to function? Isn't the system of racism essential for America to live?"

This—the idea of racism as a nebulous, omnipresent, and immutable "system" so crucial to the functioning of American society that it could never ever, ever, ever, ever possibly be defeated and therefore will never, ever, ever, ever go away completely—is the tree. Unyielding. Immovable. Not a saw on earth big enough to cut it down, and even if there was one, the roots are so deep and the soil so rich, another tree just as big would grow in its place.

And if this idea of racism seems discouraging . . . it's because it is.

But remember how earlier we briefly mentioned that many budding antiracists wind up stepping into the wrong ring? Well, in the *right* ring there's . . . a boxer. An imposing one, yes. But one that is both mortal and defeatable.

Because this is the thing: The structure of racism is just as recognizable and changeable as individual racist actions. The structure of racism isn't a tree trunk made of some unknown and indestructible substance. It's a flesh-and-blood being made up of the same sort of racist foolishness we know and recognize in the swastika tattoos of skinheads and the sharp-tipped tongues of individuals who use racial slurs. It just exists in the form of **racist policies**.

In order to succeed, we need to see our (Not-So-) Great Opponent as a *beatable* foe. And racism *is* a beatable foe. Let's revisit the definition we set at the beginning of this journey.

> **Racism:** A powerful collection of **policies** that lead to **racial inequity and injustice** that are substantiated by ideas of racial hierarchy.

And as you say in a book you'll publish in 2019, ten months before the *whole world* will witness one of the most heinous manifestations of racist violence in recent history—the death of an African American man named George Floyd at the knee (literally) of a White police officer—*Policymakers and policies make societies and institutions, not the other way around.*

Policymakers, policies, and minds are skin, blood, and bones.

Policymakers are overtakeable; they can be ousted and voted out.

Racist policies aren't fixed; they can be exposed and changed.

Individual racist minds under the influence of racist ideas can be reformed.

Really, the only people who would deny the validity of the above statements are likely to have a vested interest in *preserving* racist policymakers, policies, and ways of thinking.

So what should you *do*? Precisely what you're eventually going to:

- Confess the racist policies you support and the racist ideas you believe and express.
- Accept that you are a product of your upbringing in a nation that has racist policies based on racist ideas in its very foundations; this is the source of the racist ideas that live in you.
- Acknowledge the definition of "antiracist": someone who is supporting equitable and just policies or expressing ideas of racial equality.
- Resist the status quo and work for antiracist power and policy in the spaces you occupy.
- Recognize antiracist intersections and push back against the various blends of racism with other bigotries.
- Fight and fight and fight and fight to make antiracist ideas the fount from which all of your individual thoughts and ideas and pursuits flow.

> **Example:**
> Acquire a policymaking position; join an antiracist organization; participate in antiracist protest; give time and/or funds to support antiracist policymakers, organizations, and protest efforts aimed at shifting power and changing policy.

Easy-peasy, right?

No, obviously. If it were easy, neither this book nor the book this book came from would be necessary. But as the Irish writer Oscar Wilde said, "If it is worth attaining, it is worth fighting for."

17

THE FOUR C'S OF CHANGEMAKING: COGENCY, COMPASSION, CREATIVITY, COLLABORATION

Bam.

Mind is right.

Heart is set on making some *changes* in this often-wack world.

So what now? What *action* can you take?

The (unhelpful) answer is, it depends. Racism truly *is* like a terminal disease: It's toxic, damaging, and pervasive on the whole, but it manifests in so many different ways. Some of them are obvious—like kids hanging nooses from a tree or Uncle Buddy tossing around racial slurs at the Fourth of July picnic—but some are dastardly and insidious, camouflaging themselves or hiding behind status quo essentials, like how policing in the southern states was birthed out of slave patrols that were formed for the *sole* purpose of apprehending, terrorizing, and disciplining Black bodies, but police forces are now seen as *essential* for "maintaining safety" in communities.

NIC'S NOTES:

FYI, in not-southern states, the idea of "police"—which is derived from *polis*, the Greek word for "city"—as a formal organization designed to control "disorder" sort of originated in England. But you know we Americans like to put our own spin on things, which, in a country founded by capital-driven White men with minds packed full of racist ideas that originated in their European homelands, meant making sure

White people's money and property were protected as they continued to pursue capital gain. Enslaved and free workers had to be kept working, and assets had to be protected from *deviants*. And by this point in the book, hopefully you know who those "deviants" were perceived to be.

And can we just acknowledge how great we Americans are at euphemizing? "Law and order" might be referred to as "maintaining safety" now, but . . . policing methods haven't changed much. We'll move on now.

Which just means there's no catchall method for dealing with **racism**. No step-by-step *Here's what to do when racism reveals itself to you!*

BUT!

What you *can* do is get yourself *ready* to act. Think of it as like . . . training to become a firefighter. While it's impossible to predict how and when and where blazes will break out, a set of adaptable basic skills enables firefighters to fight—and usually put out—just about any fire.

So let's tuck four final definitions into that glorious brain of yours. Get you shored up to do some antiracist changemaking. And to keep it simple (and hopefully easy-ish to remember), like the word *change-maker*, they all begin with *C*.

cracks knuckles

First:

Cogency: The state or quality of being clear, logical, and convincing.

As you continue this journey, you're going to interact with a lot of people who are: (1) uncomfortable talking about race and/or racism and/or the intersections of racism with other bigotries, (2) "color-blind" and/or in denial about racism even being a *thing,* (3) not at all interested in eliminating racial inequities because the status quo is comfy, and/or (4) completely opposed to eliminating racism and racial inequities because they believe that's how things are *supposed* to be.

With that last group, there's not a whole lot you can do. All the cogency in the universe won't change the mind of a person who holds the core *belief* that Black people and other people of color are inferior to White people. That sort of belief doesn't actually require evidence of truth, and evidence of falsehood will be ignored or explained away. It's almost like faith.

But in a general sense, the ability to explain your position on a topic in a way that makes sense, with evidence to support your assertions, goes a long way in the push toward making an antiracist world. Which means you need to actually know what you're talking *about.* So read a ton. Research well.

Get your facts straight. Consider the types of questions you might hear from someone who isn't fully convinced of the validity of what you're presenting. *Why? How do you know? Where did you read that?* No, you can't predict EVERY possible question, but have responses to the ones *you* would ask locked and loaded so you can discuss your position with calmness and clarity.

> **NIC'S NOTES:**
> Primary sources are your friends! "What are those?" you ask? Well, they are artifacts, documents, or images that provide firsthand testimony or direct evidence concerning a topic that is the subject of research. They can be hard to find depending on the topic, but as much as you can, go straight to the source. Read old letters, laws, and speeches. Find old pictures. The internet is awesome. (Sometimes.)

> **Compassion:** Sympathetic concern for the sufferings
> or misfortunes of others.

And no, I'm not saying you need to show sympathetic concern for racists. (Though I *will* remind you that anyone who grows up in America is conditioned to believe some racist ideas by default because they are the foundations for many American social norms. **Antiracism** has to be decided upon and pursued, and it ain't an easy road, as you now know. If we're honest with ourselves, we *could* all technically empathize with people who haven't realized the existence or depth of their racist ideas and therefore haven't let them go or gotten rid of them yet. Just saying.)

You *do*, however, need to move compassionately when it comes to the sufferings and misfortunes of those on the receiving end of racism's varying manifestations. Which might sound obvious, but it's not. True compassion is feeling *with*, not feeling *for*. It's imagining yourself in the position of another and feeling the emotions as though what has happened to the other person is happening to you. And it often requires a level of vulnerability that will leave you feeling exposed and helpless—which is precisely what victims of racism and other bigotries feel All. The. Time.

Also, in many instances, moving and speaking from a place of compassion is more effective than moving and speaking from a place of anger or rage. Unless that anger/rage is shared by the audience, it puts hearers on the defensive and instantly triggers a self-protective mode that makes it difficult to listen. Compassion breeds humility, and humility makes people more likely to listen, consider, and act.

> **Creativity:** The ability to transcend traditional ideas,
> rules, patterns, or relationships and create meaningful
> new ideas, forms, methods, and/or interpretations.

This should maybe be a no-brainer, but it totally isn't: Things that are broken require parts as well as tools to get fixed, and stuff that gets tossed out completely typically needs to be replaced. This is especially true of ideologies, which govern the ways people interact with one another. Like how various forms of democracy have replaced many dictatorships and absolute monarchies. This is actually the cool thing about **antiracism**: It gives us something concrete to strive for in opposition to racism.

Creativity is vital to creating something that has never existed (at least not in these United States): a society free of racial inequities where every individual is perceived as an individual and not through the lens of faulty ideas about their racial group membership. To create this world, we have to come up with creative solutions and replacements for problematic policies. To undo mass incarceration, we have to come up with other deterrents to violence and other kinds of harm, and better approaches to rehabilitation. To eliminate racial disparities in maternal and infant mortality rates, we have to get creative about creating equitable access to good healthcare. To address ineffective—and downright life-threatening—policing techniques, we'll have to get creative with changes to training protocols, and get open to policing alternatives that will keep our communities safe *and* provide assistance to those who need it most (e.g., community-led support systems, easier access to addiction treatment, and increased mental health services).

And I know it all sounds pretty daunting, but we must never forget that *people* made the rules and created the norms in this world we currently inhabit . . . which means people can also come together to make new ones. Which leads to the final and most important *C*:

Collaboration: The process of two or more people, groups, or entities working in tandem to complete a task, produce a product, or achieve a goal.

The good news: You're already an expert at this. You literally have to be in order to survive in a world with other people in it. Getting from point A to point B in a car is an act of collaboration with all the other drivers on the road. Reading this book is an act of collaboration between you (a reader) and me (the narrator). I put the words on the page to be read; you read the words I put on the page. When you purchase or use a product, you're collaborating with the product-maker. And then, of course, there's deliberate collaboration, like on group projects.

The key here is to *use* that collaborative expertise at specific times in specific ways for specific purposes, all of which have to be agreed upon. So really, this letter-*C* word is about . . . connection, communication, and commitment (see what I did there?). Combining our different strengths—which also involves recognizing our individual weaknesses—to conceptualize and execute ideas *together*, which will have a much greater impact than anything one individual can do alone.

So how do you collaborate and who do you collaborate with? I'm sure you already know the answer: It depends. The point here is that true changemaking, though it may begin with one person, has to take root on a collective scale in order to *stick.*

Sometimes changemaking starts as seemingly small as cogently explaining to Uncle Buddy why he shouldn't use the N-word or say unkind things about immigrants. A shift in a single perspective can be an exceedingly powerful thing. One of the most cogent statements in the Bible is "Do not despise humble beginnings."

But know that grand-scale changemaking isn't only possible—it's *truly* within reach. Find some people who feel the same way you do about this sort of stuff. Then, driven by shared compassion, come together to create a cogent explanation of your position and mission, combine your varied strengths and areas of expertise, and collaborate to carry it out.

Let's get it.

- 18 -

SURVIVAL

So, I have some fantastic news and some not-so-great news.

We'll go with the former first: Remember that queen of a woman you were out on a date with when you saw that disrespectful drunk man touching a Buddha statue in a most unseemly manner? Sadiqa?

Well, she's totally into you. Like . . . *totally*. Like, you're-going-to-ask-her-to-marry-you-and-she'll-say-YES type of into you. You two will wed on a Jamaican beach in 2013 in a ceremony that will look like it's straight out of a magazine. (In fact, your wedding will wind up *in* a magazine.)

Sadly, not too long after said wedding, you'll receive your first dose of not-so-great news: In August 2013, Sadiqa will be diagnosed with stage-2 breast cancer. The good news about this not-so-great news is that Sadiqa will survive. But not without the fight of her life.

More not-so-good news: Shortly after Sadiqa's fight is over and she emerges triumphant, *Ma* will be diagnosed with stage-1 breast cancer. And *she'll* have to fight.

Ma will also survive, but over the course of those two years watching the two most important women in your life give every-thing they've got to fighting a terminal—but sometimes treatable—disease, you'll come to realize some things about racism that will challenge everything you thought to be true.

In your own words:

I became a college professor to educate away racist ideas, seeing igno-

rance as the source of racist ideas, seeing racist ideas as the source of racist policies, seeing mental change as the principal solution, seeing myself, an educator, as the primary solver.

But as you move between taking care of Sadiqa, helping Dad take care of Ma, and work, you're forced to reckon with the fact that your ideas about where racism comes from are all wrong. Which means your subsequent ideas about what to do and how to fix it . . . are wrong too.

Which is a huge deal for you. By this point, you've been studying race and racism for years. You know precisely what you believe about it. But the more you dig into the *history* of racism—because it *isn't* a thing that's been around forever—the more you realize you're going to have to make a massive paradigm shift.

What you come to discover is that racism isn't based on ignorance, as you previously presumed. It didn't come out of European people in the 1400s being ignorant about the dark-skinned individuals who occupied the continent due south of them, and then in that ignorance adhering to racist ideas that led to the creation of racist policies.

Historically speaking, racism is a function of self-interest. And of greed.

Rich and powerful policymakers, out of self-interest, created policies that would keep them rich and powerful. *Then* they cooked up racist ideas to justify and rationalize those policies. For example, the concept of slavery *far* preceded the transatlantic trade of enslaved people, but it was the Portuguese and Spanish who first primarily used *African* slave labor in their gold mines and on sugar plantations. You obviously keep more capital when you don't have to pay any salaries, so the use of *African* slave labor was appealing to *most* European countries that were getting involved with trading on a more global scale. But buying and capturing and selling other human beings for the sake of making them work without pay is deeply inhumane. So as all of this trading of enslaved people was going on, racist ideas were forming to justify the inhumanity: Africans are like beasts; they are uncivilized and amoral and savage; their bodies are obviously built for withstanding heat and working the land. So that's what they'll be forced to do.

The ignorance and hate come when everyday people consume and regurgitate these racist ideas. And so it clicks for you while watching your wife *and* your mother battle a very specific disease: The ignorance and hate are symptoms, but policy-based racism is the actual disease.

It's a powerful realization but also a daunting one. You knew that addressing ignorance and hate and replacing them with knowledge and understanding wouldn't be easy . . . but that task pales in comparison to what will be required to dismantle policy-centric racism.

But you're ready. You publish a book in 2016 about this history of racist ideas that flips your scholarly world over: *Stamped from the Beginning*. And then you take that message on the road. But the more you talk about it, the more you realize *you're* not doing a whole lot aimed at policy change. So it's time for a shift.

You come up with an excellent plan to guide your mission, first at American University in 2017, and then at the Center for Antiracist Research you'll found and direct at Boston University three years later. The plan looks like this:

- Admit racial inequity is a problem of bad policy, not bad people.
- Identify racial inequity in all its intersections and manifestations.

- Investigate and uncover the racist policies causing racial inequity.
- Formulate or find antiracist policy that can eliminate racial inequity.
- Figure out who or what group has the power to institute antiracist policy.
- Disseminate and educate about the uncovered racist policies and antiracist policy correctives.
- Work with sympathetic antiracist policymakers to institute the antiracist policy.
- Deploy antiracist power to compel or drive from power the unsympathetic racist policymakers in order to institute the antiracist policy.
- Monitor closely to ensure the antiracist policy reduces and eliminates racial inequity and injustice.
- When policies fail, do not blame the people. Start over and seek out new and more effective antiracist treatments until they work.
- Monitor closely to prevent new racist policies from being instituted.

But then, mere months after unveiling this vision and action plan, you get *another* dose of not-so-great news.

Cancer. Again.

This time in *your* body.

You being you, battling stage-4 metastatic colon cancer makes you think of racism as a cancer in the body of America. Though your cancer thankfully doesn't spread all over your body, racism permeates just about every part of America's body, intersecting with other bigotries—sexism, classism, queerphobia, ableism—and justifying obvious inequities by saying there's something wrong with the victims. It's the source of misplaced hatred and the catalyst for many mass shootings.

And it's been thriving on the self-interest and denial of policymakers and civilians alike for a long time.

Over the course of what will likely be a lifelong fight against racism, you will hear people deny racism's very existence everywhere you go. Sort of like how you were in denial about the severity of the cancer inside your own body. The truth—that you had the most serious stage and the odds suggested you would die from it—felt too big. Too much to get your mind around. You were afraid that if you faced the reality of your situation, you would see something you couldn't defeat.

The same is true of American racism. Many deny its existence because it seems far too big a foe to fell. Also, admitting that it's there necessitates some sort of action; denial means not having to *do* anything about it.

Thus, you go from making sense of racism through Sadiqa's and Ma's cancer to making sense of *your* cancer through what you understand about racism. If you can see the big bad wolf of policy and power-rooted racism as defeatable, perhaps your cancer (which carries a much lower chance of survival than Sadiqa's *or* Ma's) can be defeated too.

And it is.

Against all odds, you survive.

You survive by hanging your hat on everything that would bring you joy once you've won the fight: a long and beautiful life with your survivor wife and your daughter; interacting with the readers of your work and building a tribe of people willing to enter the antiracist fight; finishing the book *this* book is based on.

And just like you looked forward to what *could* be while fighting the third-most-deadly cancer, you imagined what this country—what the world, even—could look like without the cancer of racism. You fixed your eyes on the antiracist progress that has happened over the short span of your lifetime thus far, and you imagined it continuing on.

You fight long and hard: six months of chemotherapy followed by an invasive surgery.

And you survive. Against all odds, by the summer of 2018, your body is free of cancer.

Which is how *you* know the cancer of racism *can* be treated and obliterated. What has historically been effective at fighting racism can be likened to what has been effective at fighting cancer: Douse the status quo with the chemo or immunotherapy of antiracist policies that can shrink the racial inequity tumors and also kill the hidden racist cancer cells. What isn't destroyed that way can be cut out as long as we first admit it's there and then clearly determine what needs to go.

All is not lost for us and our society. Racist power is not a deity. Racist policies *can* be destroyed and replaced by antiracist policies. Racial inequities are *not* inevitable and *can* be eliminated.

Because racist ideas are not natural to the human mind. In the grand scope of human existence, race and racism are relatively young. Prior to the construction of race and racism in the 1400s, human beings saw colors but didn't group them into continental "races" and attach wholly made-up positive and negative characteristics to said races. That's something we *learned* to do.

And if we learned that, we can totally learn something new.

Here's to being an **antiracist**.

THE ~~END~~ BEGINNING

AFTERWORD

Yo, Nic. It's Ibram. Call me E.

Soooooo you are telling me I'm going to one day marry a woman named Sadiqa. And she's going to get breast cancer. And after she recovers, Ma's going to get cancer too. And after Ma recovers, I'm going to get colon cancer. Like, really bad cancer. The kind that kills. But I'm going to survive. And I'm going to learn about how to fight racism through these cancer battles.

Sorry, I'm just, like, shocked. I'm seventeen years old, and I don't be in the hospital like that here in Manassas, Virginia, in 1999. Well, I did go to the emergency room when I broke my wrist playing basketball when we lived in Queens, New York. Had a blue cast signed by my friends. I broke my right wrist, so I practiced dribbling, shooting layups, and passing with my left hand. Nothing was going to keep me away from basketball.

I think I was in eighth grade. You know, the class with Kwame. And you are right: his jokes hit differently. I had no idea I was expressing racist ideas about African immigrants—just as African immigrants were expressing racist ideas about African Americans. I had no idea about ethnic racist ideas. I didn't know "not racist" was not a thing. I had no idea about a lot of things in this book.

I didn't realize the racial problem was . . . What's the word you used? Structural. I didn't know racism was about power and policy and ideas. In school and on TV, I've learned about the "White only" signs and a little about slavery. But that was back in the day. I thought everything was cool now. I didn't think everybody was cool. I thought there were individual racists, like the cops who like to pull me over.

I have a black Honda Civic. My license plate is ESRIDE. I must admit, though, I do speed sometimes. I'm sorry. It's dangerous. I'm slowing down. I could hurt somebody, especially myself, since I'm still learning how to drive. But Hollywood should make a movie based on drag racing. I think it would be mad popular! Because we fast and we furious, especially when we get pulled over by cops. They don't have to roll up on me like I stole something, like I'm armed or something. I always wondered why they all scared of me. But when I'm rolling with one of my White friends and they get pulled over, the cops are cool. Bodily racist ideas are real. People keep acting like I'm dangerous. But now I know what's dangerous are those racist ideas that Black and Brown boys like me are dangerous. Thank you.

I don't leave my house until ten or fifteen minutes before the bell rings. School starts at around 7:30 a.m. I speed to get to school on time, but I'm late, like, every day. I leave so late because I don't like school, which you already know. I'm not popular or anything. I'm shy. I don't really feel like I'm that smart. At least that's how many teachers and students treat me. I thought I brought that mistreatment onto myself. Because I don't apply myself, as my parents say. But I do think if people thought more highly of me, then I'd think more highly of myself. Then again, I should have never allowed what other people think of me to impact what I think of myself. I should not internalize their racist ideas about me. I'm going to stop that.

After all, you're telling me I'm going to college! And you're telling me I actually love learning—that school isn't my problem, that what and how I'm learning is the problem. And you're telling me I love learning so much, I'm going to become a college professor! And you're telling me I'm going to write books! And you're telling me the book you wrote to me and young people in your time is based on a book I wrote in the future (but before the future you wrote this in). I don't be reading like that now, and you're telling me I be writing like that in the future! That's wild. That's really wild. I'm still in shock. I don't know whether I'm more shocked about all of that stuff or all the cancer.

I just didn't see any of this in my future. You know, that's the beauty of the future. Speaking of the future, thank you for sending this book to the past. I should probably ask you: How did you do it? It's dated 2023. I'm reading it at the end of 1999. How did you send this book back twenty-four years through time to me? It is like some *Back to the Future*–type stuff? Do they have time machines in the future? I watched *The Matrix* this year—and that movie got me thinking all types of stuff. And you know, in a few months, the millennium is going to end. People all scared. I'm not scared. I'm just curious. Is sending things back to the past on the other side of the millennium?

You have great timing. I mean, great timing. I entered this Martin Luther King Jr. oratorical contest at my high school a few days ago. I had just walked into my room, popped on a basketball game on the TV, and sat down at my desk. The game in the background settled my nerves because the oratorical competition is tomorrow morning and I have to finish my speech. We're supposed to speak on *"What would be Dr. King's message for the millennium?"* I want the speech to be good. My parents give speeches all the time as ministers. I want to make my parents proud. They haven't been proud of me much lately.

After I finished my first draft, I felt like I needed something. I looked over at my small bookcase. I didn't expect to see any books that could help me. I saw all the yellow CliffsNotes and my handful of books on basketball. Then I got a glimpse of the book you sent me. The spine caught my eye. *How to Be a (Young) Antiracist* was just waiting for me like a basketball on a court. I picked it up. Sat down in my desk chair, rested back, and started reading it. The game faded away as I read. I didn't stop until I finished it.

The more I read it, the more I realized how bad I needed it. Like, *BAD* BAD. I was about to bomb this speech. Like, really embarrass myself and Black people—and I had no idea.

You had me face myself like nobody's business. It was hard looking in the mirror and seeing all those ugly things I thought about Black people, and eventually White people too. And now that I think about it, I look down on Asian people and Indigenous people and Middle Eastern people and all the increasing numbers of Latin Americans in Manassas, Virginia. What I thought was true about racial groups are actually racist ideas about racial groups . . . That blew my mind!

But you are telling me that we don't face ourselves just to face ourselves. After we face ourselves, we are supposed to face the world. We put the mirror away and pull out the microscope to see the racial inequities and injustices around us. All the White authors and subject matters in our schools. All the Indigenous peoples poorer than White people. All the Black teens incarcerated at the highest rates. All the money that politicians spend on prisons and police instead of schools and teachers. All the White immigrants being welcomed and Latino immigrants being deported. You are saying that when we see all this racial inequity and injustice, we are seeing racism. And we should come to see how racism intersects with sexism, queerphobia, classism, ableism, and colorism.

I have to tell you: Kaila and Yaba sound intimidating. But on the real, my Aunt Jeanette is intimidating. She tells it like it is, tells people off when they warrant it, and I love her for it. Yaba and Kaila sound like Aunt Jeanette. I wish, though, Kaila and Yaba were in my high school. They could have schooled me earlier. But now I have the opportunity to school myself about sexism and queerphobia.

And colorism. I won't be getting those colored contacts I've been wanting to get. Thank you for saving me from that silliness of trying to look White. My brown eyes are where it's at. And don't worry, Nic, I'm going to push back against the idea that the lighter, the better. I'm going to stop clowning my dark-skinned friend Brandon as "night train" and "Black and Decker." I'll be alert for when guys in my school be saying, "She cute for a dark-skin girl." I know that's colorism now. And I won't overreact by not dating light-skinned girls in college. Just because racist ideas favor Light people and even White people, that doesn't mean I have to disfavor them.

To create justice, I have to be about justice. Once I've faced myself and my world, I have to start making power moves to change myself and my world. Being antiracist is a journey, not an end goal. Reading books like *How to Be a (Young) Antiracist* can be a starting point. But I learn by doing. Being antiracist is kind of like being a basketball player who has to play both defense and offense as part of a team. I can't do it alone. We have to defend against racist violence, against racial inequity. But if we only play defense, we will never win our freedom from racism. We have to play offense too, putting in place antiracist power and policy that deconstruct the power and policy structure of racism. That's how we flip this joint over! That's how we win equity and justice for the people! This book got me hyped!

Sorry for being over the top. It's late, past midnight. The basketball game has long since ended. I think my parents and my brother are asleep. I'm tired, but at the same time I feel like I'm waking up. I'm ready, Nic. I'm ready to begin my journey to be antiracist.

I started with this MLK speech. I just finished rewriting it. Let me know what you think.

You know where I was going to say, "Now, one hundred thirty-five years later, the Negro is still not free . . . Our youth's minds are still in captivity!"

I rewrote that to "Now, one hundred thirty-five years later, the Negro is still not free . . . Black people are still in captivity to racism!"

You know where I had "Black youth think it's okay to be those who are most feared in our society!"?

I dropped that for "Racist ideas make Black youth the most feared in our society!"

You know where I was going to shout, "Black youth think it's okay not to think!"?

I remixed that to "Racist ideas got people thinking Black youth don't be thinking!"

You know the line that said, "Black youth think it's okay to climb the high tree of pregnancy!"?

The new line is "Racist America thinks it's okay to climb the high tree of injustice!"

You know where I was saying, "Black youth's minds are being held captive, and our adults' minds are right there beside them. Because they somehow think that the cultural revolution that began on the day of my dream's birth is over"?

I changed that to "American minds are being held captive to racist ideas. Because they somehow think that the antiracist revolution that began long ago is over."

After reading that book, I literally sat here and rewrote the entire MLK speech.

You know where I had "How can it be over when our kids leave their houses not knowing how to make themselves, only knowing how to not make themselves?"?

I now have "How can it be over when our kids leave their houses not having the opportunity to make themselves, only the racism to not make themselves?"

And then I closed this way: "So I say to you, my friends, that even though this antiracist revolution may never be over,

"I still have a dream . . .

"I still have a dream that you and I—that we—in this new millennium, will be antiracist and do the impossible. If we can abolish slavery in the nineteenth century, if we can abolish parts of Jim Crow in the twentieth century, then we can abolish racism once and for all in the twenty-first century."

NIC STONE'S ACKNOWLEDGMENTS

It is safe to say that this book has stretched me more than anything I've ever written, and the first person I need to thank is Jason Reynolds for continuing to do stuff that makes me want to stretch. I was sitting with him in a Decatur, Georgia, restaurant when he told me he was adapting *Stamped from the Beginning*, and it immediately lit a fire in me to do something similar, because when it comes to Jason, I am a huge copycat. Then I have to thank reading and social studies educator extraordinaire Michael Bonner, who was the first person I told, "I think I want to adapt *How to Be an Antiracist* for young people." Mr. Bonner's initial push and belief that I could bring the idea to fruition truly carried me from initial inquiry through first-pass pages. Thanks also to Nigel Livingstone for his continued on-the-ground support that got me through a number of dark nights of the soul, and for his superb management of our children so that I could chase these dreams. Also to Wyatt Oroke, educator extraordinaire and my primary reader and sounding board who helped me to make sure this adaptation is not only readable, but also teachable: forever indebted to you, homie. And to the team of queens who literally made this happen: Mollie Glick, Ayesha Pande, Namrata Tripathi, and Zareen Jaffery. Which leads me to the GOAT: Dr. Ibram X. Kendi. Thank YOU, IXK, for not only doing epic, society-shifting work, but also NOT looking at me sideways when I slid into your Instagram DMs asking you to put me on the list of potential candidates if you wanted *How to Be an Antiracist* adapted for young readers, responding almost immediately to be like, "Absolutely. Let me alert the publisher," and then trusting me wholeheartedly with your work to bring this book to life. Thank you for allowing me to join this journey that has also been life changing for ME.

IBRAM X. KENDI'S ACKNOWLEDGMENTS

I want to first and foremost acknowledge the young people who are striving to be antiracist. Your voice, your actions, your intelligence, your courage inspired us to create this book with care and conviction. And love. And let me take this opportunity to share my love and appreciation for my partner, Sadiqa, and our daughter, Imani.

I must also share my appreciation and gratitude for one of the best writers doing it: Nic Stone. The liveliness of your writing and your personality, your out-of-the-box literary voice, your audacity and boldness and brilliance—it has been an absolute gift for me to work with you and learn from you. When you slid up in my DMs, you were already in my heart as the one. As the one who could remix *How to Be an Antiracist* for young people like no other. And you did! You created a book like no other. And I couldn't be more thankful. Just as I couldn't be more thankful to Namrata Tripathi and Zareen Jaffery at Kokila for their intrepid championing and stewardship of this book. I couldn't be more thankful to my colleagues at the Boston University Center for Antiracist Research, especially Adeline Gutierrez Nunez, Hunter Moyler, Tami Nguyen, and of course Heather Sanford, who helped ensure the accuracy of this book. And as always, Ayesha Pande, I am grateful for your rock-solid support. I am proud of the work we've done together over the years. I am filled right now with pride for this wonder, with thanks for all the hands that made it, with joy for all the hands that will remake the world with it.

ENDNOTES

BEGINNING IN THE MIDDLE:
YOUR (RACIST) INTRODUCTION

p. 8 this tends to happen . . . anyone realizing it For more on this idea, see Ibram X. Kendi, "The Heartbeat of Racism Is Denial," *The New York Times,* January 13, 2018, available at nytimes.com/2018/01/13/opinion/sunday/heartbeat-of-racism-denial.html.

1. DEFINITIONS: WHY THEY MATTER
(JUST LIKE BLACK LIVES DO)

p. 13 [Skinner] was growing in popularity For explanatory pieces on Skinner's life and influence and role in Urbana 70, see James Earl Massey, "The Unrepeatable Tom Skinner," *Christianity Today,* September 12, 1994, available at christianitytoday.com/ct/1994/september12/4ta011.html; and Edward Gilbreath, "A Prophet Out of Harlem," *Christianity Today,* September 16, 1996, available at christianitytoday.com/ct/1996/september16/6ta036.html.

p. 14 a couple of Tom Skinner's books See Tom Skinner, *How Black Is the Gospel?* (Philadelphia: Lippincott, 1970); and Tom Skinner, *Words of Revolution: A Call to Involvement in the Real Revolution* (Grand Rapids, MI: Zondervan, 1970).

p. 14 Soul Liberation was up first For a remembrance of this evening with Soul Liberation playing and Tom Skinner preaching that is consistent with Dr. Kendi's parents' memories, see Edward Gilbreath,

Reconciliation Blues: A Black Evangelical's Inside View of White Christianity (Downers Grove, IL: InterVarsity Press, 2006), 66–69.

p. 14 prepping the crowd for what Skinner would say For the audio and text of Tom Skinner's sermon at Urbana 70 entitled "The U.S. Racial Crisis and World Evangelism," see urbana.org/message/us -racial-crisis-and-world-evangelism.

p. 15 for the liberation of Black people For a good book on the philosophy of Black theology, see James H. Cone, *Risks of Faith: The Emergence of a Black Theology of Liberation, 1968–1998* (Boston: Beacon Press, 2000).

p. 15 the Black Power movement For an overview of Black Power, see Peniel E. Joseph, *Waiting 'Til the Midnight Hour: A Narrative History of Black Power in America* (New York: Henry Holt, 2007).

p. 16 *Black Theology & Black Power* James H. Cone, *Black Theology & Black Power* (New York: Seabury, 1969).

p. 18 In early 2022, 74 percent of White families lived in houses they owned These figures can be found in U.S. Census Bureau, "Quarterly Residential Vacancies and Home Ownership, First Quarter 2022," April 27, 2022, Table 7, available at census.gov/housing/hvs /files/currenthvspress.pdf.

p. 18 nearly six years longer than that of Black People Elizabeth Arias, Betzaida Tejada-Vera, Kenneth D. Kochanek, and Farida B. Ahmad, "Provisional Life Expectancy Estimate for 2021," *Vital Statistics Rapid Release*, Report No. 23, August 2022, 3, available at cdc.gov /nchs/data/vsrr/vsrr023.pdf.

p. 18 the infant mortality rate of Black babies is double that of White babies See CDC, "Infant Mortality," September 8, 2021, available at cdc.gov/reproductivehealth/maternalinfanthealth/infantmortality.htm

p. 18 African Americans are 33 percent more likely to die from cancer See Rebecca L. Siegel, Kimberly D. Miller, and Ahmedin

Jemal, "Cancer Statistics, 2022," *CA: A Cancer Journal for Clinicians* 72, no. 1 (January / February 2022), doi.org/10.3322/caac.21708.

p. 18 Racist idea See Ibram X. Kendi, *Stamped from the Beginning: The Definitive History of Racist Ideas in America* (New York: Nation Books, 2016).

p. 18 "The blacks . . . body and mind" Thomas Jefferson, *Notes on the State of Virginia* (Boston: Lilly and Wait, 1832), 150.

p. 21 "We have *all* . . . as equals" Audre Lorde, "Age, Race, Class, and Sex: Women Redefining Difference," in *Sister Outsider: Essays and Speeches* (Freedom, CA: Crossing Press, 1984), 115.

p. 25 "You do not take a person . . . completely fair" For a full video of President Johnson's speech at Howard, see "Commencement Speech at Howard University, 6/4/65. MP2265-66.," TheLBJLibrary, available at youtube.com/watch?v=vcfAuodA2x8.presidency.ucsb.edu/documents/commencement-address-howard-university-fulfill-these-rights

p. 26 The Regents of the University of California voted to end Affirmative Action Phillip Carter, "Regents end UC affirmative action policies," *Daily Bruin*, July 23,1995, available at dailybruin.com/1995/07/23/regents-end-uc-affirmative-act.

p. 26 . . . decline in the admission Jamillah Moore, *Race and College Admissions: A Case for Affirmative Action* (Jefferson, NC: McFarland & Company, Inc. Publishers, 2005), 26–27.

p. 26 which are proven to boost scores by hundreds of points See Abigail Johnson Hess, "Rich Students Get Better SAT Scores – Here's Why," CNBC, October 3, 2019, available at cnbc.com/2019/10/03/rich-students-get-better-sat-scores-heres-why.html.

p. 27 "In order to get beyond . . . treat them differently" For his full dissent, see Harry Blackmun, Dissenting Opinion, *Regents of the Univ. of Cal. v. Bakke, 1978,* C-SPAN Landmark Cases, available at landmarkcases.c-span.org/Case/27/Regents-Univ-Cal-v-Bakke.

2. OF TWO MINDS: DUELING CONSCIOUSNESS

p. 29 "the year when this country . . . war on crime" Elizabeth Hinton, "Why We Should Reconsider the War on Crime," *Time,* March 20, 2015, available at time.com/3746059/war-on-crime-history/.

p. 29 President Richard Nixon's War on Drugs in 1971 "President Nixon Declares Drug Abuse 'Public Enemy Number One,'" Richard Nixon Foundation, June 17, 1971, available at youtube.com /watch?v=y8TGLLQlD9M.

p. 29 some *hefty* allegations Dan Baum, "Legalize It All: How to Win the War on Drugs," *Harper's Magazine,* April 2016, available at harpers.org/archive/2016/04/legalize-it-all/.

p. 30 Ronald Reagan doubled down Ronald Reagan, "Remarks on Signing Executive Order 12368, Concerning Federal Drug Abuse Policy Functions," in *Public Papers of the Presidents of the United States: Ronald Reagan, 1982* (Washington, DC: U.S. Government Printing Office, 1982), 813.

p. 30 American prison population *quadrupled* See Fox Butterfield, "Study Finds Big Increase in Black Men as Inmates Since 1980," *The New York Times,* August 28, 2002, available at nytimes .com/2002/08/28/us/study-finds-big-increase-in-black-men-as -inmates-since-1980.html.

p. 30 Black and Latinx people wound up *wildly* over-represented John Gramlich, "The Gap Between the Number of Blacks and Whites in Prison Is Shrinking," Pew Research Center, January 12, 2018, available at pewresearch.org/fact-tank/2018/01/12/shrinking -gap-between-number-of-blacks-and-whites-in-prison/.

p. 30 drug use rates are about the same National Center for Behavioral Statistics and Quality, *Racial/ethnic Differences in Substance Use, Substance Use Disorders, and Substance Use Treatment Utilization among People Aged 12 or Older (2015-2019)* (Rockville, MD: Substance Abuse and Mental Health Services Administration, 2021),13, available at samhsa

.gov/data/sites/default/files/reports/rpt35326/2021NSDUHSUChart book102221B.pdf.

p. 30 glaring racial inequity in drug arrest numbers Jonathan Rothwell, "Drug Offenders in American Prisons: The Critical Distinction Between Stock and Flow," Brookings, November 25, 2015, available at brookings.edu/blog/social-mobility-memos/2015/11/25/drug-offenders-in-american-prisons-the-critical-distinction-between-stock-and-flow/.

p. 30 require police to make more drug arrests in order to secure more funding Michelle Alexander, *The New Jim Crow: Mass Incarceration in the Age of Colorblindness* (New York: The New Press, 2012), 73.

p. 31 are more likely to *sell* drugs than Black people Keegan Hamilton, "The War on Drugs Remains as Racist as Ever, Statistics Show," Vice, March 14, 2017, available at vice.com/en/article/7xwybd/the-war-on-drugs-remains-as-racist-as-ever-statistics-show.

p. 31 low-income areas where drug transactions were more likely to take place out in the open See Leonard Saxe, Charles Kadushin, Andrew Beveridge, David Livert, Elizabeth Tighe, David Rindskopf et al, "The Visibility of Illicit Drugs: Implications for Community-Based Drug Control Strategies," *American Journal of Public Health* 91, no. 12 (December 2001): 1987–1994.

p. 32 was (and still is) disproportionately White See Christopher Pulliam, Richard V. Reeves, and Ariel Gelrud Shiro, "The Middle Class Is Already Racially Diverse," Brookings, October 30, 2020, available at brookings.edu/blog/up-front/2020/10/30/the-middle-class-is-already-racially-diverse/.

p. 34 highest number of individuals receiving government assistance . . . Kathryn Cronquist, *Characteristics of Supplemental Nutrition Assistance Program Households: Fiscal Year 2019* (U.S. Department of Agriculture, Alexandria, VA, 2021), 25, available at fns-prod.azureedge

.us/sites/default/files/resource-files/Characteristics2019.pdf; and Kaiser Family Foundation, "Distribution of the Nonelderly with Medicaid by Race/Ethnicity, 2019," available at kff.org/medicaid/state-indicator /medicaid-distribution-nonelderly-by-raceethnicity/?currentTimeframe =0&sortModel=%7B%22colId%22:%22Location%22,%22sort%22:%22 asc%22%7D.

p 34 White people made up 75.8 percent of the total US population in 2019 available at census.gov/quickfacts/fact/table/US /RHI125221

p. 36 assimilate, "to acquire the traits held in esteem by the dominant white Americans" Gunnar Myrdal, *An American Dilemma: The Negro Problem and Modern Democracy* (New York: Harper, 1944), 2:929.

3. POWER (AKA: THE THING THAT MAKES RACE A THING)

p. 37 Black folks wanted to keep *their* *good* kids away For some of the early research on this issue, see Diana T. Slaughter and Barbara Schneider, "Parental Goals and Black Student Achievement in Urban Private Elementary Schools: A Synopsis of Preliminary Research Findings," *The Journal of Intergroup Relations* 23, no. 1 (Spring/August 1985), 24–33; and Diana T. Slaughter and Barbara Schneider, *Newcomers: Blacks in Private Schools* (Evanston, IL: Northwestern University School of Education, 1986).

p. 40 Prince Henry the Navigator of Portugal Ibram X. Kendi, *Stamped from the Beginning: The Definitive History of Racist Ideas in America* (New York: Nation Books, 2016), 22–25.

p. 40 buying and selling to African bodies exclusively Martin Meredith, *The Fortunes of Africa: A 5000-Year History of Wealth, Greed, and Endeavor* (New York: PublicAffairs, 2014), 93–94; Gomes Eanes de Zurara, *The Chronicle of the Discovery and Conquest of Guinea* (London: Hakluyt Society, 1896).

p. 40 first transcribed account of perceived Black inferiority
Ibid., xii.

p. 40 "lost" (from a Christian perspective), living "like beasts, without any custom of reasonable beings" Ibram X. Kendi, *Stamped from the Beginning: The Definitive History of Racist Ideas in America* (New York: Nation Books, 2016), 22–25; and Zurara, *The Chronicle of the Discovery and Conquest of Guinea*, 1:85–86.

p. 41 *negros da terra* Mieko Nishida, *Slavery & Identity: Ethnicity, Gender, and Race in Salvador, Brazil, 1808–1888* (Bloomington, IN: Indiana University Press, 2003), 13.

p. 41 "strong for work . . . undemanding tasks" Zuazo quoted in David M. Traboulay, *Columbus and Las Casas: The Conquest and Christianization of America, 1492–1566* (Lanham, MD: University Press of America, 1994), 58.

p. 41 color-code the "races" Dorothy Roberts, *Fatal Invention: How Science, Politics, and Big Business Re-create Race in the Twenty-First Century* (New York: New Press, 2011), 252–53.

p. 41 . . . "Vigorous, muscular." Carl Linnaeus, *Systema Naturae*, 10th ed., (Stockholm: Laurentius Salvius, 1758), 1:21–22.

p. 42 bypass Muslim traders of enslaved people For literature on this history, see Robert C. Davis, *Christian Slaves, Muslim Masters: White Slavery in the Mediterranean, the Barbary Coast, and Italy, 1500–1800* (New York: Palgrave Macmillan, 2003); Matt Lang, *Trans-Saharan Trade Routes* (New York: Cavendish, 2018); and John Wright, *The Trans-Saharan Slave Trade* (New York: Routledge, 2007).

p. 42 making *mad* money for King Alfonso Gabriel Tetzel and Václáv Sasek, *The Travels of Leo of Rozmital, 1465–1467,* translated by Malcolm Letts (Cambridge: Hakluyt Society at the University Press, 1957).

4. BIOLOGY

p. 45 Black students are twice as likely . . . See Renee Ryberg, Sarah Her, Deborah Temkin, and Kristen Harper, "Despite Reductions Since 2011–2012, Black Students and Students with Disabilities Remain More Likely to Experience Suspension," Child Trends, August 9, 2021, available at childtrends.org/publications/despite-reductions-black -students-and-students-with-disabilities-remain-more-likely-to-experience -suspension.

p. 47 disproportionately applied to Black and Brown kids "Are We Closing the School Discipline Gap?" The Center for Civil Rights Remedies, UCLA, available at civilrightsproject.ucla.edu/resources /projects/center-for-civil-rights-remedies/school-to-prison-folder /federal-reports/are-we-closing-the-school-discipline-gap/Are WeClosingTheSchoolDisciplineGap_FINAL221.pdf.

p. 48 "more natural physical ability" John Hoberman, *Darwin's Athletes: How Sport Has Damaged Black America and Preserved the Myth of Race* (New York: Houghton Mifflin Harcourt, 1997), 146.

p. 48 "One drop of Negro blood makes a Negro" Thomas Dixon, *The Leopard's Spots: A Romance of the White Man's Burden, 1865–1900* (New York: Doubleday, 1902), 244.

pp. 48–49 "certain inherited abilities . . . astronomy" Dinesh D'Souza, *The End of Racism: Principles for a Multiracial Society* (New York: Free Press, 1996), 440–41.

p. 49 Black men have large penises William Lee Howard, "The Negro as a Distinct Ethnic Factor in Civilization," *Medicine* 9 (June 1903), 423–26.

p. 49 Curse of Ham See George Best, *A True Discourse of the Late Voyages of Discoverie* (London: Henry Bynneman, 1578).

p. 49 polygenesis See Isaac de La Peyrère, *Men Before Adam* (Amsterdam, 1655) per Britannica britannica.com/topic/Prae-Adamitae.

p. 49 shut down by scientific principles See Charles Darwin, *The Origin of Species* (London: John Murray, 1859), 6.

p. 49 "survival of the fittest" Herbert Spencer, *The Principles of Biology* (London: Williams and Norgate, 1864), 1:444–45.

p. 49 three possible fates for the "weaker" races Albion W. Small and George E. Vincent, *An Introduction to the Study of Society* (New York: American Book Company, 1894), 179.

p. 50 "[I]n . . . 99.9 percent the same" The White House, Office of the Press Secretary, "Remarks Made by the President . . . on the Completion of the First Survey of the Entire Human Genome Project," National Human Genome Research Institute, June 26, 2000, available at genome.gov/10001356/.

p. 50 segregationist interpretation of the research See Nicholas Wade, "For Genome Mappers, the Tricky Terrain of Race Requires Some Careful Navigating," *The New York Times,* July 20, 2001, available at nytimes.com/2001/07/20/us/for-genome-mappers-the-tricky-terrain -of-race-requires-some-careful-navigating.html.

p. 50 assimilationist interpretation jumped on the notion of "sameness" Ken Ham, "There Is Only One Race—The Human Race," *The Cincinnati Enquirer,* September 4, 2017, available at cincinnati.com /story/opinion/contributors/2017/09/04/there-only-one-race-human -race/607985001/ Also see Ken Ham and A. Charles Ware, *One Race One Blood: A Biblical Answer to Racism* (Green Forest, AR: Master Books, 2010).

p. 51 Chester Pierce was defining a new term: *microaggression* Chester Pierce, "Offensive Mechanism," in *The Black Seventies,* ed. Floyd B. Barbour (Boston, MA: Porter Sargent, 1970), 280.

p. 51 "brief, everyday exchanges . . . group membership" Derald Wing Sue, *Microaggressions in Everyday Life: Race, Gender, and Sexual Orientation* (Hoboken, NJ: Wiley, 2010), 24.

p. 52 Gaslighting . . . "psychological . . . reality" "Gaslighting,"

Merriam-Webster, accessed September 8, 2022, available at merriam
-webster.com/dictionary/gaslighting/.

p. 52. the compounded psychological results Sherri Gordon,
"What Is Gaslighting?" Verywell Mind, July 25, 2022, available at
verywellmind.com/is-someone-gaslighting-you-4147470.

5. BEHAVIOR

**p. 55 Proslavery theorists attributed these behavioral "defi-
ciencies" to freedom.** Philip A. Bruce, *The Plantation Negro as a Free-
man: Observations on His Character, Condition, and Prospects in Virginia*
(New York: G. P. Putnam's Sons, 1889), 48, 242, 53, 129, 16, 42–43, 212,
3–4.

**p. 55 attributed the supposed "crippled" intellects, darkened
minds . . .** William Lloyd Garrison, "Preface," in *Frederick Douglass,
Narrative of the Life of Frederick Douglass, an American Slave* (Boston:
Anti-Slavery Office, 1849), vii.

**p. 55 Black people on the whole are prone to behave a certain
way** Jason L. Riley, *Please Stop Helping Us: How Liberals Make It Harder
for Blacks to Succeed* (New York: Encounter Books, 2015), 4.

p. 56 using the words of Dr. King to shame the kids See
Paul Duggan, "D.C. Residents Urged to Care, Join War on Guns," *The
Washington Post*, January 14, 1995, available at washingtonpost.com
/archive/local/1995/01/14/dc-residents-urged-to-care-join-war-on
-guns/0b36f1f3-27ac-4685-8fb6-3eda372e93ac/.

p. 56 you've let down *everybody* Black See James Forman Jr.,
Locking Up Our Own: Crime and Punishment in Black America (New York:
Farrar, Straus and Giroux, 2017), 195.

**p. 57 achievement gap between Black students and basically
everyone else** For this data in the Nation's Report Card, see nations
reportcard.gov/.

p. 57 test-prep course See Sean Teehan, "New SAT Paying Off for Test-Prep Industry," *The Boston Globe,* March 5, 2016, available at bostonglobe.com/business/2016/03/04/new-sat-paying-off-for-test-prep-industry/blQeQKoSz1yAksN9N9463K/story.html.

p. 58 people can do better on it . . . a little green See Mark Sherman, "Why We Don't Give Each Other a Break," *Psychology Today,* June 20, 2014, available at psychologytoday.com/us/blog/real-men-dont-write-blogs/201406/why-we-dont-give-each-other-break.

p. 58 "proceed with an accelerating rate as the racial admixture becomes more and more extensive" Carl C. Brigham, *A Study of American Intelligence* (Princeton, NJ: Princeton University Press, 1923), 210.

6. BLACK (AKA: THE CHAPTER WHERE WE START TALKING ABOUT THE N-WORD)

p. 62 *negars*—was found in the journal of John Rolfe See Linton Weeks, "Anatomy of a Word," The *Washington Post*, December 11, 2001, available at washingtonpost.com/archive/lifestyle/2001/12/11/anatomy-of-a-word/0d499dd4-bb6f-4bb9-a132-50420c41ceec/.

p. 62 "status of a husband was that of a slave" See "Darwin on marriage," Darwin Correspondence Project, accessed June 8, 2022, available at darwinproject.ac.uk/tags/about-darwin/family-life/darwin-marriage

p. 62 "a person of any racial or ethnic origin" Dictionary.com, accessed September 8, 2022, available at dictionary.com/browse/nigger.

p. 63 Black comedians who lean on these See Chris Rock, *Bring the Pain*, HBO, June 1, 1996, available at youtube.com/watch?v=coC4t7nCGPs.

p. 65 Black officers have been involved James Forman Jr., *Locking Up Our Own: Crime and Punishment in Black America* (New York: Farrar, Straus and Giroux, 2017), 107–8.

7. WHITE

p. 71 terminate Affirmative Action programs See Peter T. Kilborn, "Jeb Bush Roils Florida on Affirmative Action," *The New York Times,* February 4, 2000, available at nytimes.com/2000/02/04/us /jeb-bush-roils-florida-on-affirmative-action.html.

p. 71 joined the majority of Black Floridians in voting to save the rest of America from the Bush family "How Groups Voted in 2000," Roper Center for Public Opinion Research, available at ropercenter.cornell.edu/how-groups-voted-2000.

p. 72 Al Gore's face fills the screen See Peter Marks, "The 2000 Elections: The Media; A Flawed Call Adds to High Drama," *The New York Times,* November 8, 2000, available at nytimes.com/2000/11/08/us /the-2000-elections-the-media-a-flawed-call-adds-to-high-drama.html.

p. 72 a *very* narrow lead See David Barstow and Don van Natta Jr., "Examining the Vote; How Bush Took Florida: Mining the Overseas Absentee Vote," *The New York Times,* July 15, 2001, available at nytimes .com/2001/07/15/us/examining-the-vote-how-bush-took-florida -mining-the-overseas-absentee-vote.html.

p. 72 his brother's appointees are overseeing the recount Lisa Getter, "Jeb Bush's Recount Role Examined," *Los Angeles Times,* July 14, 2001, available at latimes.com/archives/la-xpm-2001-jul-14-mn-22362 -story.html.

p. 72 Black people all over the state were prevented from voting For example, see Linda Meggett Brown, "FAMU Students Protest Election Day Mishaps in Florida," *Diverse: Issues in Higher Education,* December 6, 2000, available at diverseeducation.com /article/1034/; and Jerry White, "Florida A&M Students Describe Republican Attack on Voting Rights," *World Socialist Web Site,* December 6, 2000, available at wsws.org/en/articles/2000/12/flor-d06.html.

p. 72 11 percent of registered voters . . . purge list See Ari Berman, "How the 2000 Election in Florida Led to a New Wave of Voter

Disenfranchisement," *The Nation,* July 28, 2015, available at thenation
.com/article/archive/how-the-2000-election-in-florida-led-to-a-new
-wave-of-voter-disenfranchisement/

**p. 72 close to one hundred and eighty thousand ballots
were invalidated in a race won by fewer than six hundred
votes.** Greg Palast, "1 Million Black Votes Didn't Count in the 2000
Presidential Election," *San Francisco Chronicle,* June 20, 2004,
available at sfgate.com/opinion/article/1-million-black-votes-didn
-t-count-in-the-2000-2747895.php; and Doyle McManus, Bob Drogin,
and Richard O'Reilly, "Bush Wins, Gore Wins -- Depending on How
Ballots Are Added Up," *Chicago Tribune,* November 13, 2001,
available at chicagotribune.com/news/sns-ballots-story.html.

**p. 72 two thousand students complete a silent march to the
Capitol** See Brown, "FAMU Students Protest Election Day Mishaps
in Florida" and White, "Florida A&M Students Describe Republican
Attack on Voting Rights."

p. 73 source of *their* alleged "devil" nature See Elijah Muhammad, *Message to the Blackman in America* (Chicago: Muhammad Temple
No. 2, 1965).

**p. 73 evil scientist . . . take revenge by creating "upon the
earth a devil race"** Ibid.

p. 73 "these blond, pale-skinned, cold blue-eyed devils"
Malcolm X and Alex Haley, *The Autobiography of Malcolm X* (New York:
Random House, 2015), 190–94.

p. 74 "hell torn by quarreling and fighting" Ibid.

p. 74 The two-cradle theory See Cheikh Anta Diop, *The Cultural
Unity of Negro Africa: The Domains of Patriarchy and of Matriarchy in Classical Antiquity* (Paris: Présence Africaine, 1962).

p. 75 product of its rearing in the Ice Age See Michael Bradley,
*The Iceman Inheritance: Prehistoric Sources of Western Man's Racism,
Sexism and Aggression* (Toronto: Dorset Publishing, Inc.,1978).

p. 75 **Frances Cress Welsing . . . "profound sense of numerical inadequacy and color inferiority"** Frances Cress Welsing, *The Isis Papers: The Keys to the Colors* (Paris: Présence Africaine, 1962).

8. COLOR

p. 81 **FAMU's legendary marching band** For a history, see Curtis Inabinett Jr., *The Legendary Florida A&M University Marching Band: The History of "The Hundred"* (New York: Page Publishing, 2016).

p. 82 **Brief background on blackface** Ayanna Thompson, "Blackface Is Older Than You Might Think," *Smithsonian Magazine*, April 29, 2021, available at smithsonianmag.com/arts-culture/blackface-older -you-think-180977618/.

p. 82 **Eurocentrism in light-skinned blackface** Margaret L. Hunter, *Race, Gender, and the Politics of Skin Tone* (New York: Routledge, 2013), 57.

p. 83 **Colorism, a term coined by . . . Alice Walker** See Alice Walker, *In Search of Our Mothers' Gardens: Womanist Prose* (San Diego, CA: Harcourt Brace Jovanovich, 1983), 293.

p. 83 **light-skinned enslaved people typically working in the house** See William L. Andrews, *Slavery and Class in the American South: A Generation of Slave Narrative Testimony, 1840–1865* (New York: Oxford University Press, 2019), 102.

p. 83 **Enslavers even *paid* more for light-skinned women** Walter Johnson, *Soul by Soul: Life Inside the Antebellum Slave Market* (Cambridge, MA: Harvard University Press, 1999), 150–56.

p. 83 **In fact, dark-skinned "field slaves" were said to have bodies that "are, generally, ill-shaped" and hair that was "the farthest removed from the ordinary laws of nature"** See Samuel Stanhope Smith, *An Essay on the Causes of the Variety of Complexion and Figure in the Human Species* (Philadelphia: Robert Aitken, 1787), 57–58, 32.

p. 83 **Light people . . . tend to receive better treatment** See Matthew S. Harrison and Kecia M. Thomas, "The Hidden Prejudice in Selection: A Research Investigation on Skin Color Bias," *Journal of Applied Social Psychology* 39, no. 1 (January 2009).

p. 84 Light people worked . . . distance themselves from Dark people Willard B. Gatewood, *Aristocrats of Color: The Black Elite, 1880–1920* (Bloomington: Indiana University Press, 1990), 157–63.

p. 84 inequities between Light and Dark people persist See Heather Timmons, "Telling India's Modern Women They Have Power, Even Over Their Skin Tone," *The New York Times,* May 30, 2007, available at nytimes.com/2007/05/30/business/media/30adco.html.

p. 84 China to India to the Philippines to Brazil See "Mercury in Skin Lightening Products," News Ghana, June 13, 2012, available at newsghana.com.gh/mercury-in-skin-lightening-products/.

p. 85 photography project created by Brazilian artist See Fiona Macdonald, "The artist who reveals our Pantone shades," BBC Culture, Nov. 7, 2017, available at bbc.com/culture/article/20171107 -the-artist-who-reveals-our-pantone-shades.

9. ETHNICITY

p. 88 Abner Louima See Jim O'Grady and Beth Fertig, "Twenty Years Later: The Police Assault on Abner Louima and What it Means," WNYC News, August 9, 2017, available at wnyc.org/story/twenty-years -later-look-back-nypd-assault-abner-louima-and-what-it-means-today/.

p. 88 Amadou Diallo See Beth Roy, *41 Shots . . . and Counting: What Amadou Diallo's Story Teaches Us About Policing, Race, and Justice* (Syracuse, NY: Syracuse University Press, 2009).

p. 90 some French enslavers preferred the Congolese See Hugh Thomas, *The Slave Trade: The Story of the Atlantic Slave Trade, 1440–1870* (New York: Simon & Schuster, 2013), 399.

p. 90 favored captives from Senegambia Ibid.

p. 90 partial to ethnic groups from what is now Ghana Ibid., 400.

p. 90 *most* traders . . . valued Angolans the least Ibid., 402.

p. 91 Black immigrants . . . viewed African Americans See Mary C. Waters, *Black Identities: West Indian Immigrant Dreams and American Realities* (Cambridge, MA: Harvard University Press, 1999), 138.

p. 91 African Americans were prone to categorizing Black immigrants Ibid., 69.

p. 91 Chinese Exclusion Act of 1882 For anti-Asian immigration violence and policies, see Beth Lew-Williams, *The Chinese Must Go: Violence, Exclusion, and the Making of the Alien in America* (Cambridge, MA: Harvard University Press, 2018); and Erika Lee, *The Making of Asian America: A History* (New York: Simon & Schuster, 2015).

p. 91 limited immigrants from Africa . . . *and* Asia "Who Was Shut Out?: Immigration Quotas, 1925–1927," *History Matters: The U.S. Survey Course on the Web*, available at historymatters.gmu.edu/d/5078.

p. 92 "We should have more people from places like Norway" See Trump quoted in Sarah Ruiz-Grossman, "People on Twitter Tell Trump No One in Norway Wants to Come to His 'Shithole Country,'" *HuffPost*, January 11, 2018, available at huffingtonhuffpost.com/entry/trump-shithole-countries-norway_n_5 a58199ce4b0720dc4c5b6dc.

p. 92 "created really the solid middle class of America" "The American People Are Angry Alright . . . at the Politicians," Steve Bannon interviews Jeff Sessions, SiriusXM, October 4, 2015, available at soundcloud.com/siriusxm-news-issues/the-american -people-are-angry.

p. 92 Anti-Latinx, anti–Middle Eastern, and anti-Black immigration policies enacted during this period Jessica Bolter, Emma Israel, and Sarah Pierce, "Four Years of Profound Change: Immigration Policy during the Trump Presidency" (Washington, D.C.: Migration Policy Institute, 2022), available at migrationpolicy.org/research/four -years-change-immigration-trump.

p. 92 Cuban . . . immigrants being viewed more favorably than . . . Mexican peoples See Brittany Blizzard and Jeanne Batalova, "Cuban Immigrants in the United States," Migration Policy Institute, June 11, 2020, available at migrationpolicy.org/article/cuban-immigrants-united-states.

p. 92 East Asian immigrants . . . viewed more favorably than . . . South Asian peoples See Ellen D. Wu, *The Color of Success: Asian Americans and the Origins of the Model Minority* (Princeton, NJ: Princeton University Press, 2014).

p. 95 didn't think of the ethnic group B person as "their own people" John Thornton, *Africa and Africans in the Making of the Atlantic World, 1400–1800*, 2nd ed. (New York: Cambridge University Press, 1998), 99.

10. BODY

p. 97 predominantly White For a good study on the transformation in New York City, see Walter Thabit, *How East New York Became a Ghetto* (New York: NYU Press, 2005).

p. 98 "Blacks must understand . . . A Black face" "Transcript of President Clinton's Speech on Race Relations," CNN, October 17, 1995, available at cnn.com/US/9510/megamarch/10-16/clinton/update/transcript.html.

p. 99 viewed as "creatures" Hugh Drysdale quoted in Mary Miley Theobald, "Slave Conspiracies in Colonial Virginia," *Colonial Williamsburg*, Winter 2005–2006, available at research.colonialwilliamsburg.org/foundation/journal/winter05-06/conspiracy.cfm

p. 99 "ruthless savages" "A Declaration of the Causes Which Impel the State of Texas to Secede from the Federal Union," Texas State Library and Archives Commission, February 2, 1861, available at tsl.texas.gov/ref/abouttx/secession/2feb1861.html.

p. 99 "poor African" . . . **"wild beast seeking whom he may devour"** Tillman quoted in Albert B. Hart, *The Southern South* (New York: D. Appleton, 1910), 93.

p. 100 drastic changes in youth punishment policies See Ann Devroy, "Crime Bill Is Signed with Flourish," *The Washington Post,* September 14, 1994, available at washingtonpost.com/archive /politics/1994/09/14/crime-bill-is-signed-with-flourish/650b1c2f -e306-4c00-9c6f-80bc9cc57e55/.

p. 100 still disproportionately impact Black and Brown teenagers Ranya Shannon, "3 Ways the 1994 Crime Bill Continues to Hurt Communities of Color," Center for American Progress, May 10, 2019, available at americanprogress.org/article/3-ways-1994-crime-bill-continues -hurt-communities-color/.

p. 100 "Black inner-city neighborhoods" John DiIulio, "The Coming of the Super-Predators," The Weekly Standard, November 27, 1995, available at washingtonexaminer.com/weekly-standard/the coming-of-the-super-predators.

p. 100 "Most inner-city children grow up surrounded by" William J. Bennett, John J. DiIulio, Jr., and John P. Walters, *Body Count: Moral Poverty . . . And How to Win America's War Against Crime and Drugs* (New York: Simon & Schuster, 1996), 28.

p. 100 "A new generation of street criminals is upon us" Ibid., 26.

p. 100 "[R]adically impulsive, brutally remorseless youngsters" Ibid., 27.

p. 100 violence had begun to decline (dramatically) and homicides were at their lowest rate since the 1980s. See Rashawn Ray and William A. Galston, "Did the 1994 Crime Bill Cause Mass Incarceration," Brookings, August 28, 2020, available at brookings.edu /blog/fixgov/2020/08/28/did-the-1994-crime-bil-cause-mass -incarceration/; and Disaster Center, "United States Population and

Number of Crimes, 1960– 2019," disastercenter.com/crime/uscrime
.htm.

**p. 102 there *are* more recorded instances of violent harm in
"urban" majority-Black neighborhoods** See Rachel E. Morgan and
Alexandra Thompson, "Criminal Victimization, 2020," Bureau of Justice Statistics, U.S. Department of Justice, October 2021, 10, available at
bjs.ojp.gov/sites/g/files/xyckuh236/files/media/document/cv20.pdf.

**p. 102 the relationship between low-income/high-unemploy-
ment rates** Delbert S. Elliott, "Longitudinal Research in Criminology:
Promise and Practice," paper presented at the NATO Conference on
Cross-National Longitudinal Research on Criminal Behavior, July
19–25, 1992, Frankfurt, Germany; and Austin Nicholas, Josh Mitchell,
and Stephan Lindner, *Consequences of Long-Term Unemployment* (Washington, D.C.: Urban Institute, 2013), 1.

**p. 103 Rates of violence tend to be far lower in middle and
upper-income majority-Black neighborhoods** HUD USER, "Neighborhoods and Violent Crime," Evidence Matters, Summer 2016, huduser
.gov/portal/periodicals/em/summer16/highlight2.html.

**p. 103 mass shootings in the United States are carried out
by White people** The Violence Project, "Why Are Almost All Mass
Shooters Men?" The Violence Project, March 29, 2021, theviolence
project.org/media/why-are-almost-all-mass-shooters-men/

11. GENDER

p. 106 Intersectionality Kimberlé Crenshaw, "Mapping the Mar-
gins: Intersectionality, Identity Politics, and Violence Against Women of
Color," *Stanford Law Review* 43, no. 6 (July 1991), 1242.

p. 107 Gender racism Dr. Kendi's definition of this term was
inspired by Philomena Essed's definition of "gendered racism" See
Philomena Essed, *Understanding Everyday Racism: An Interdisciplinary
Theory* (Newbury Park, CA: SAGE, 1991), 31.

p. 109 Black women with some college education make just $29 more per week U.S. Department of Labor, Women's Bureau, "Women's Median Weekly Earnings by Educational Attainment, Race, and Hispanic Ethnicity (Annual)," 2020, available at dol.gov/agencies /wb/data/earnings/Women-median-weekly-earnings-educational -attainment-race-Hispanic-ethnicity.

p. 109 Black women have to earn graduate degrees Ibid.

p. 109 The race-gender with the highest average income U.S. Bureau of Labor Statistics, "Usual Weekly Earnings of Wage and Salary Workers, First Quarter 2022," news release, April 15, 2022, Table 2, bls .gov/news.release/archives/

p. 109 Black and Native women experience poverty at a higher rate See Robin Bleiweis, Diana Boesch, and Alexandra Cawthorne Gaines, "The Basic Facts about Women in Poverty," Center for American Progress, August 3, 2020, americanprogress.org/article /basic-facts-women-poverty/.

p. 109 Black women are three times more likely to die Centers for Disease Control and Prevention, "Working Together to Reduce Black Maternal Mortality," April 6, 2022, available at cdc.gov/healthequity /features/maternal-mortality/index.html.

p. 109 Black girls are over three times more likely to be incarcerated The Sentencing Project, "Incarcerated Women and Girls," May 12, 2022, 5, available at sentencingproject.org/publications/incarcerated -women-and-girls/.

p. 109 The birth rate among Black and Latina teens is more than double that of White girls. Centers for Disease Control and Prevention (CDC), "About Teen Pregnancy," November 15, 2021, available at cdc.gov/teenpregnancy/about/index.htm.

p. 109 earn $0.64 and $0.57 respectively for every $1.00 paid to White men with the *exact same credentials* Robin Bleiweis, Jocelyn Frye, and Rose Khattar, "Women of Color and the Wage Gap," Center for American Progress, November 17, 2021, available at american progress.org/article/women-of-color-and-the-wage-gap/.

p. 110 the Combahee River Collective See Keeanga-Yamahtta Taylor, ed., *How We Get Free: Black Feminism and the Combahee River Collective* (Chicago: Haymarket Books, 2017).

p. 110 "To be recognized as human . . . " Combahee River Collective Statement, April 1977, quoted in Ibid., 19.

12. ORIENTATION

p. 114 Black gay men are *less* likely to have unprotected sex . . . use illicit drugs See Jacob Anderson-Minshall, "What's At The Root of the Disproportionate HIV Rates for Black Men?," *Plus*, March 6, 2017, available at hivplusmag.com/stigma/2017/3/06 /whats-root-disproportionate-hiv-rates-their-queer-brothers.

p. 114 *most* Black gay men do *not* contract HIV Ibid.

p. 116 To be antiracist, *all* Black lives have to matter to you See Foluké Tuakli and Chandelis R. Duster, "Black Lives Matter Movement Awarded Sydney Peace Prize for Activism," NBC News, November 2, 2017, available at nbcnews.com/news/nbcblk/black-lives-matter -movement-awarded-sydney-peace-prize-activism-n816846.

13. CLASS

p. 119 the most dangerous neighborhoods in Philadelphia And they are still being told this. See Nick Johnson, "The 10 Worst Neighborhoods In Philadelphia For 2022," RoadSnacks, April 6, 2022, available at roadsnacks.net/worst-philadelphia-neighborhoods/.

p. 119 the origins of *ghetto.* For the following, see Mitchell Duneier, *Ghetto: The Invention of a Place, the History of an Idea* (New York: Farrar, Straus, and Giroux, 2016).

p. 120 *Dark Ghetto* Kenneth B. Clark, *Dark Ghetto: Dilemmas of Social Power* (New York: Harper & Row, 1965).

p. 121 "White trash" See Nancy Isenberg, *White Trash: The 400-Year Untold History of Class in America* (New York: Viking, 2016).

p. 122 an ethnographic study of Mexican families Oscar Lewis, *Five Families: Mexican Case Studies in the Culture of Poverty* (New York: Basic Books, 1959).

p. 122 "People with a culture of poverty" Oscar Lewis, "The Culture of Poverty," *Trans-action 1* (1963), 17–19.

p. 122 "We've got this tailspin . . . culture of work" Ryan quoted in Zak Cheney-Rice, "Paul Ryan's Racist Comments Are a Slap in the Face to 10.5 Million Americans," *Mic,* March 13, 2014, available at mic.com/articles/85223/paul-ryan-s-racist-comments-are-a-slap-in-the-face-to-10-5-million-americans.

p. 122 What began as redlining in the 1930s See Richard Rothstein, *The Color of Law: A Forgotten History of How Our Government Segregated America* (New York: Liveright Publishing Corporation, 2017).

14. CULTURE

p. 126 languages created by enslaved Africans in European colonies See John Baugh, *Out of the Mouths of Slaves: African American Language and Educational Malpractice* (Austin: University of Texas Press, 1999); Barbara Lalla and Jean D'Costa, *Language in Exile: Three Hundred Years of Jamaican Creole* (Tuscaloosa: University of Alabama Press, 1990); Arthur K. Spears and Carole M. Berotte Joseph, eds., *The Haitian Creole Language: History, Structure, Use, and Education* (Lanham, MD: Lexington Books, 2010); Steven Byrd, *Calunga and the Legacy of an African Language in Brazil* (Albuquerque: University of New Mexico Press, 2012); and John M. Lipski, *A History of Afro-Hispanic Language: Five Centuries, Five Continents* (Cambridge, UK: Cambridge University Press, 2005).

p. 126 African American Ebonics Robert L. Williams, *History of the Association of Black Psychologists: Profiles of Outstanding Black Psychologists* (Bloomington, IN: AuthorHouse, 2008), 80. Also see Robert

L. Williams, *Ebonics: The True Language of Black Folks* (St. Louis, MO: Institute of Black Studies, 1975).

p. 127 European-based cultures at the top Gunnar Myrdal, *An American Dilemma: The Negro Problem and Modern Democracy* (New York: Harper, 1944), 2:928–29.

p. 130 "All cultures must be judged . . . any single culture" Ashley Montagu, *Man's Most Dangerous Myth: The Fallacy of Race,* 2nd ed. (New York: Columbia University Press, 1945), 150.

15. SPACE

p. 135 "The rejection . . . intellectual struggle" Molefi Kete Asante, *Afrocentricity* rev. ed. (Trenton, NJ: Africa World Press, 1988), 104.

p. 137 seven of the eight Ivy League universities were founded between available at bestcolleges.com/blog/history-of-ivy-league/

p. 137 HBCUs . . . don't represent "the real world" Evelyn Diaz, "Hold Up: Aisha Tyler Thinks HBCUs Are Bad for Black Students?," BET, April 28, 2016, available at bet.com/celebrities/news/2016/04/28 /aisha-tyler-slams-hbcus.html.

p. 138 When the ruling was handed down that segregated schools *Brown v. Board of Education of Topeka*, 347 U.S. 483 (1954), available courtesy of Cornell Law School's Legal Information Institute at law.cornell.edu/supremecourt/text/347/483%26gt#writing -ZS.

16. FAILURE → SUCCESS

p. 143 The "white tree" American Civil Liberties Union (ACLU), "Background: Jena 6," available at aclu.org/other/background-jena-6.

p. 144 Six Black Students—including a star football player —beat up a White kid For a good interview that details the case, see "The Case of the Jena Six: Black High School Students Charged with Attempted Murder for Schoolyard Fight After Nooses Are Hung from Tree," *Democracy Now,* July 10, 2007, available at democracynow.org/2007/7/10/the_case_of_the_jena_six.

p. 145 voter registration laws that disproportionately limit voters of color, particularly Black voters "The Impact of Voter Suppression on Communities of Color," Brennan Center for Justice, January 10, 2022, available at brennancenter.org/our-work/research-reports/impact-voter-suppression-communities-color.

p. 149 racist minds didn't change until after racist policies did Lawrence D. Bobo, Camille Z. Charles, Maria Krysan, and Alice D. Simmons, "The Real Record on Racial Attitudes," in *Social Trends in American Life: Findings from the General Social Survey Since 1972,* ed. Peter V. Marsden (Princeton, NJ: Princeton University Press, 2012), 47.

p. 150 "If it is worth attaining . . . " "The Death of Oscar Wilde," Squaducation, available at quaducation.com/blog/death-oscar-wilde.

p. 151 policing in the southern states was birthed out of slave patrols See Sally E. Hadden, *Slave Patrols: Law and Violence in Virginia and the Carolinas* (Cambridge, MA: Harvard University Press, 2003).

p. 151 the idea of "police" Jean-Paul Brodeur, Thomas Whetstone, William Francis Walsh, Michael Parker Banton, and George L. Kelling, "Police," *Encyclopedia Britannica,* December 17, 2021, available at britannica.com/topic/police.